I0046453

Succeeding as a Young Entrepreneur

Succeeding as a Young Entrepreneur

Lessons in Life and Business

Harvey Morton

BEP

BUSINESS EXPERT PRESS

Leader in applied, concise business books

Succeeding as a Young Entrepreneur: Lessons in Life and Business

Copyright © Business Expert Press, LLC, 2024

Cover design by Out Of Box Ltd

Interior design by Exeter Premedia Services Private Ltd., Chennai, India

All rights reserved. No part of this publication may be reproduced, stored in a retrieval system, or transmitted in any form or by any means—electronic, mechanical, photocopy, recording, or any other except for brief quotations, not to exceed 400 words, without the prior permission of the publisher.

First published in 2023 by
Business Expert Press, LLC
222 East 46th Street, New York, NY 10017
www.businessexpertpress.com

ISBN-13: 978-1-63742-537-4 (paperback)
ISBN-13: 978-1-63742-538-1 (e-book)

Business Expert Press Business Career Development Collection

First edition: 2023

10 9 8 7 6 5 4 3 2 1

Dedicated to my wonderful parents, Clair and John and my brilliant sister Megan.

Description

Succeeding as a Young Entrepreneur: Lessons in Life and Business describes Harvey Morton's inspirational journey from being bullied at school, told by teachers that he would never succeed, to winning his first business award when he was 15 years old. Later, becoming an ambassador for Youth Employment UK, and going on to work with a long list of well-known brands. Including Sheffield Hallam University, Alton Towers, and the BBC.

He has won several prestigious awards, like the IPSE National Young Freelancer of the Year award in 2018. Supported by a circle of family and friends, business connections, and those who wanted to see him follow his dream of becoming a self-employed business owner.

The importance of being passionate about the career you choose and giving back when you can, to make a difference in others' lives, is highlighted. While continuing to work hard toward achieving your goals. Irrespective of how many times you fail, or become discouraged by negativity. Similarly, the necessity of assessing every risk you take, learning how to do what you need to, and not ignoring self-development. So that you can take advantage of opportunities, and eventually create your own.

Until you truly are... *an entrepreneur.*

The lessons in life and business which Harvey Morton shares in *Journey of a Young Entrepreneur* are an essential first step on the path to success.

Along with the realization, that the only limits we have, are those we impose on ourselves.

Keywords

starting a business; start-up; small business ideas; online business ideas; young entrepreneur; young businessman; entrepreneurship; entrepreneur; best business starting books; business ideas for young adults; I want to start a business but have no ideas

Contents

Testimonials

"Harvey is a powerhouse of ideas and ambition, and his new read-in-a-day book will help uplift any budding entrepreneur – young or old – to follow in his impressive footsteps. Written with warmth, honesty, and humor, it's a delightful read to get you started in business."—**Jane Hamilton, Sunemployment Editor**

"Packed with practical tips on how to succeed and delivered with the enthusiasm to inspire the next generation of entrepreneurs."—**IPSE (Association for Independent Professionals and the Self-Employed)**

"This is a great read for any young entrepreneur or potential entrepreneur. Its strengths lie in the focus on down-to-earth practical tips in every chapter combined with Harvey himself. He writes straight from the heart, and is totally open about his experiences to date, good and bad. When you read that in combination with what he has achieved, it will inspire anyone that they too can overcome obstacles, that they too can move towards their dream. Heart-warming, inspirational and honest. Highly recommended."
—**Jan Cavelle, Author**

"A truly insightful read, Harvey's story should be an inspiration to all of us. This book, full of practical tips and thoughtful personal insight, is a must read for everyone."—**Laura-Jane Rawlings, CEO at Youth Employment UK**

"This book is a real inspiration about how to succeed and use every advantage that you can – the hints and tips that Harvey shares throughout the book are invaluable. In the book he recognizes that there are different pathways which you can take, as not everyone needs to be an entrepreneur, but can think like one which is an important differentiation. If you use this book as a starting guide, you won't go wrong, as Harvey has already lived these life experiences."—**Sharon Blyfield OBE, Head of Early Careers and Apprenticeships GB at Coca-Cola Europacific Partners**

"This book is a gem for any young people/adults looking at starting a business. Harvey speaks openly and honestly about struggles at school and offers practical hints and tips throughout the book for business and at times about life. Extremely digestible, the content will work well for all type of readers and the nature of the chapters allows you to dive in and dive out where required."
—**Ben Dyer, Award-Winning Entrepreneur**

Acknowledgments

Thank you to everyone who has helped me along the way, and to all my amazing friends for cheering me on, you all know who you are and I'm so grateful for all that you do.

Helen Campbell, thank you for coming to rescue me when I felt so burnt out from all the pressures of freelancing in 2019 and for helping me to find my direction again. Your guidance, support, kindness, and encouragement have been outstanding.

Morgan Killick, I truly value your insight and guidance. Thank you for supporting me on my journey writing this book and for all your reassurance when I doubted myself.

Ellen Beardmore, for all your infectious enthusiasm in supporting the launch of my book and helping me to secure lots of brilliant press coverage.

David Grey MBE, for encouraging me from day one and lifting me when I was at the lowest point in my life, helping me to get back on track again.

Laura Jane Rawlings, Lauren Mistry, and the entire team at Youth Employment UK for allowing me to volunteer with you and giving me a voice to speak about lots of the issues that are so important to me. You've changed my life and given me so many skills, I'll always be grateful for everything you've done for me, and I can't wait to continue supporting your work.

Rob King and Caroline Nouvellon, for being my cheerleaders during my time at Sheffield Hallam University and giving me so many opportunities to excel and grow. Without you both, I wouldn't be where I am today.

Pennie Raven and Jonny Douglas, for helping me to craft my perfect business pitch and giving me a huge confidence boost when I needed it the most.

Paulette Edwards, for your kindness, and warmth and for always allowing me to share my story in my own words whenever I've been on your radio program. I feel so lucky to know you, you're a hugely talented broadcaster.

Chikumo Fiseko, for all your generous words of wisdom and for always providing a listening ear whenever I need it. We might be miles apart, but I know that whenever we do see each other it's always like picking up where we left off.

Nelly Naylor and Beth Jasmine Blake, for your kind-heartedness, and consideration and for always encouraging me to reach all my goals.

Max Scotford and Luisa Van Der End, I feel so lucky to be able to call you both friends. Thank you for your backing and for keeping me together with your amazing company and positivity.

Annabel Peake, for your friendship and for continuing to encourage me to keep on writing, you're amazing!

Jackie Goodrum, Jo Silverwood, and all the great staff at Meadowhead School who encouraged me to get started with my business and allowed me to keep going in the years that followed alongside my studies—I don't have the words to describe what you did for me and the impact you had. And to all my lecturers and tutors at Sheffield Hallam University for your passion and guidance.

Jo Roberts, and everyone at The Ryegate Children's Centre in Sheffield for working with me from such a young age to overcome my difficulties and for inspiring me to believe I could be anything I wanted to be when others told me what I couldn't be.

Finally, to my parents Clair and John and my sister Megan for bearing with me while I've poured so many hours into this book and for everything you've done for me. I'm so incredibly lucky to have such a brilliant family.

PART 1

Introduction

CHAPTER 1

The Importance
of Being Me

In this section, build the character to be an entrepreneur and make some important early choices about who you are as a person.

I am a young entrepreneur, and I am not who you think I am.

You hear entrepreneur, and you see someone dripping in confidence who breezed through school and is the popular one who attracts the love interest in the best Hollywood fashion.

I am not this person. If I had been this person, I probably wouldn't be an entrepreneur.

I was born in January 1998 in Sheffield, UK, with periventricular leukomalacia. It means my eyes don't work together, and I have a tremor. My hand-eye coordination is weak, so I find sports challenging and struggle to navigate uneven surfaces. You can imagine how the clumsy kid in glasses did at school. I was bullied a lot!

Fortunately, I had brilliant parents, Clair and John, who helped me form some fantastic memories. My sister Megan, born in November 1999, is my best friend and has always been my partner in crime.

My parents are essential to my success, so I want to use this as the first lesson on how to be an entrepreneur. You need to look for the role models around you.

Both my parents worked hard. My mum juggled multiple jobs, sacrificing her career to be there for my sister and me. My dad was self-employed, though he swapped his business for a job with much more security when his children were born. Money was sometimes tight, though I would have never known it as a child. They taught me the most important lesson, to be grateful for everything there rather than being upset about what isn't.

My parents were content and happy no matter what the external pressures were because they were grateful for what they did have. By being given this lesson in gratitude, I can use it in good and bad times and make the best of everything that comes my way.

My parents also brought our family dog into the home. I learned so many lessons from Jess, who is sadly no longer with us. This dog showed me how important it was to be in the present and follow your instincts. It might sound strange, an entrepreneurial book suggesting you get a pet, but don't underestimate the lessons you can learn from everything around you.

I count myself lucky for the life I enjoyed at home. Very lucky.

I wasn't so lucky at school.

Primary school between the age of 4 and 11 started well. While I wasn't given the support I needed to cope with my additional needs, I did well because I was relatively academic. I was never at the top of the class but always did well enough not to raise concerns. I felt largely ignored and expected to get on with things.

As I was forced to do physical education despite my difficulties with coordination, I was put in some challenging situations. These situations were the root of much of the bullying I experienced, which began about two years before the end of primary school.

Children are cruel and do not know the harm they do. Yet, we should not underestimate the damage done by bullying. I was called names because I wore glasses and my voice was mimicked. I spoke a lot slower than most people and was made to feel conscious of this by the other children. I was kicked and pushed, and things were thrown at me. During football, I was the target because it was funny how I flinched when the ball was heading my way. I had no chance of dealing with it any other way, as my condition made it impossible to coordinate a better response. The kids weren't to know, and it impacted me anyway.

I was miserable, and my confidence was lost. I was nervous and fragile, and there was a lot of concern about my entry into secondary school at the age of 11. I had lost my voice, and I wanted to hide.

Fortunately, as is the case in all the best success stories, I met a teacher at secondary school who was a guardian angel, Jackie Goodrum. She pushed me in the right direction, was warm and supportive, and allowed me to work out how to be confident in this new environment. She gently pushed me onto the residential trip so I could experience being away from home for the first time. While I was worried about being away from my haven and being bullied, I learned that I could do most things despite what others might say or do. This trip was my first step in finding myself, as I realized what I could do if I stepped outside my comfort zone. I was aware that I needed the support of Mrs. Goodrum and the support worker, Will Allen, but I also knew I had to have brought courage to have done so well.

The bullying was persistent through secondary school, though I had learned that I was up to the challenge it posed. I knew I could do things that I had thought impossible before. When you lack coordination and still go abseiling and take on archery, as I did on this residential trip, I can handle a few silly comments.

Then, something happened that changed everything.

I entered a competition called the BiG Challenge. Teams from schools and colleges were given £25 to set up a business and run it across two terms. I was excited. The idea of making money while still at school was brilliant. Gabe, my closest friend, set up a business with me to sell a range of keyrings and greeting cards with caricatures of popular celebrities and film stars.

While some teachers questioned if I had the confidence to succeed in the competition, Mrs. Goodrum made sure I had the same chance as everyone else. She put me in touch with the school's enterprise coordinator, Jo Silverwood. Mrs. Silverwood saw my ambition and work ethic and mentored me through the competition. She appreciated what I brought and didn't consider what I might lack, so Gabe and I pushed forward with our business idea.

We won the best presentation to the judges and third prize in our year group category. Imagine a boy who had been painfully bullied because of the way he spoke, and I was part of a team that won the best presentation to the judges. I was hooked.

I may not have won the competition, but I received two mentors in my life who were far better prizes! I met David Grey MBE, the chair of the competition, who took me under his wing and was the best cheerleader. I had another role model. The second person I met was Pete Eason, who helped Gabe and me understand what it took to build a business and how to build my confidence.

I later entered the BiG Challenge again with my business, which offered IT support to individuals and businesses. I had to work hard to overcome the prejudices of people who thought I was too young to offer IT support. I succeeded.

Getting Past the Doubts

I started when I was young and faced constant challenges because of my age. People wondered at my experience and my capacity to deliver on what I promised.

David Grey encouraged me to attend networking events, even though I was always the youngest there by at least 10 years. I found it incredibly daunting, as I was still in school. The thought of walking into a room of grown-ups and presenting myself and my business ideas made me nervous. It was at these networking events that I made some brilliant contacts, some of whom have become great friends.

However, I need some resilience at these events too. I found some people that I met there to be quite snobby and pompous, and it was always a challenge to get others even to acknowledge that I was there. There were sniggers and laughs, and sometimes my business pitch was easily dismissed. You've got to take others' opinions of you with a pinch of salt in these situations; otherwise, they could easily eat away at you.

Networking involves making connections not only with likely customers or clients but also with other individuals who might refer business to you or mention your name in some positive way to people they know.

Top tips:

- Bring your business cards with you.
- Pay attention to your appearance because people will be looking at you from across the room. First impressions count for a lot.
- Prepare a brief "elevator speech," introducing yourself and your business. This will be especially helpful if you're nervous about meeting new people.
- Avoid the trap of spending your time with people you know. Make an effort to speak to new people.
- Focus on what you can do for others, not what they can do for you.

I always made an effort to thank anyone I had met after a networking event (and still do)! It makes a difference. If you enjoyed chatting with someone, let them know and suggest ways you could work with them in the future. Life, in general, is all about making connections. When you are in business, you never know when these connections are going to prove helpful. Therefore, spare the time to make people feel special.

Takeaways

- Learn to be grateful for what you have.
- Find your mentors and role models and learn from them.
- If it's hard, do it anyway.

CHAPTER 2

Could You Be an Entrepreneur Too?

In this section, assess if being self-employed and running a business is the right choice for you.

There are two things I didn't tell you about me. First, I have always been fascinated by technology, and I enjoy figuring out how to use things. As I wasn't able to go to sports clubs with my friends, I ended up spending a lot of time on my own on the computer. Second, I have always wanted to work in radio. I know the slow-speaking kid who has the ambition to be in radio doesn't bode well. I would spend hours creating my shows and schedules and reading out the singles charts to my parents (did I tell you what good people they were?).

Now, why are these two details important? Well, they tell you a little about my passions. Part of the reason I am a successful entrepreneur is that I worked on projects that meant a lot to me.

I was also fortunate to undertake some marketing placements as part of my college enrichment program. I learned that my IT business would be better focused on offering digital marketing services, including web design, social media management, and copywriting. I say fortunate, but again I followed my interests and so was engaged enough to learn everything I could from these experiences.

Now, here is the secret that no one tells you about self-employment. It might be scary and hard work, but you always get to do the work that interests you the most. Think about it. I used to do this stuff on my computer as a hobby when I was a kid, and now I charge people to do it for them.

Before we go any further, I want you to decide if this is the right step for you. If I know anything, it is that we are all different. So, before I encourage you to do something, let's check if it's the right thing.

What Does Self-Employed Mean?

At the most basic level, being self-employed means being your boss. You choose when you work and whom you work with. Independence is great, and you know if you put in the hard work, you are fully in control of your success. You will be free of all that office politics that makes your friends miserable, and with the right sort of work ethic and attitude, your earning potential is much higher.

However, you have to consider the benefits of employment too. Being employed gives you security. You will sign a contract, which is your safety net, as you know you will have money coming in. Your contract will also tell you exactly what is expected of you, which you will have to decide if you are self-employed. You will also get paid annual leave, sick leave, and a pension scheme, and your employer will sort out your tax for you. It also means that you can switch it off when you are not at work. If you are self-employed, your passion is likely going to consume your home life, too, if you aren't disciplined enough.

Being Self-Aware

Deciding if you want to be self-employed is like any career move; you need to weigh up the pros and cons before you act. The best way to assess if you as an individual should be self-employed is to undertake a strength, weakness, opportunity, threat (SWOT) analysis. This is not only a great business tool in general but also a way of identifying your strengths and weaknesses, and then assessing the opportunities you bring to your life and the threats posed.

Strengths are the positive characteristics that help you toward your goals. I have resilience and understand the importance of gratitude.

Weaknesses are those things about you that hold you back from your goals. I can sometimes flinch away from a challenge.

Opportunities are aspects of your life and character that improve your situation. I met my role models and mentors early, and I recognized who these were.

Threats are aspects of your character that negatively impact your prospects. I speak slowly, and I need to keep pushing past this if I want to continue to build my business.

It is important to step back and be objective when completing your SWOT analysis. Be specific about the aspects you will bring to being an entrepreneur. While you might feel embarrassed about your weaknesses, there is no need to be. These weaknesses are also opportunities to learn and the chance to improve your chances of success if you do something about them. The point of this analysis is to help you make a decision about being self-employed, and it will help you see what you need to do to maximize your chances of success.

I didn't know about SWOT analysis when I started my IT business; I just spotted an opportunity. There were a lot of companies offering help and advice to businesses but nothing to the consumer. The Business to Business (B2B) market was saturated, but the Business to Consumer (B2C) market was open for someone to build a business, so I set up a website and got started. It helped that I was motivated by the competition. As I was only 15, there was a significant threat to my success. Had I known about this, I might not have gotten started, and I would have missed the opportunity I spotted.

So, while doing a SWOT analysis is a great idea, it is also not meant as a barrier to what feels right to you. I knew I could do the job I was hired to do, and I went about proving that my age was no barrier. I built a solid reputation and began getting more business. Awareness is great, and if you know what you have within you to overcome any threats or weaknesses, go with your gut instincts. Remember what I learned from Jess, my dog? You have got to live life in the present and do what feels right today.

Why do I suggest doing a SWOT analysis for your career if I didn't? Probably that I would have acted much more consciously if I had understood my strengths and weaknesses. I might have better avoided some of the threats and made more of the opportunities.

If your instincts tell you that being an entrepreneur, a SWOT analysis shouldn't deter you. What it will do is raise your awareness of how to act more strategically and grow your business more easily and, potentially, quicker.

Building Resilience to Follow Your Passion

Protecting your mental health while starting as an entrepreneur is essential. You can be consumed with building your success and forget to maintain a work–life balance. Therefore, you need a safe haven, a place where you can escape and where your business is no longer important or the center of your attention. I didn't do this well, at first, and found myself overwhelmed. I was struggling to keep up with the demands.

I made a decision a while back to make a conscious effort to protect my mental health. I began writing about it on my blog, helping others with this too. In some respects, the bullying I experienced at school prepared me well for escaping pressure. I found a love of films while I was at school and would often go to the cinema. This is still a place I can go as my haven away from the pressures of my work.

You might find that the way to avoid burnout is to have coffee with friends or take part in sports. A safe haven is a place where you can go and do something other than your business. Even when you take on a passion as a business, you need something else so your mind, body, and spirit can relax.

Conclusion

So, deciding to be an entrepreneur is a bold choice. I feel it is important that I point out some key points about my journey that influenced me and might have an influence on you.

1. I followed a passion. From a young age, I was fascinated by technology, and I wanted to work in the radio industry. I loved doing this work enough to make it my hobby. Therefore, when it was tough to get going, and people didn't trust 15-year-old me as much as I hoped when offering technical support, it was worth pushing through because I loved what I was doing. I would have been doing it anyway, even if I didn't get paid.

2. I went to Sheffield Hallam University and studied Business and Enterprise Management, so I could learn what it takes to build a business. I had something up and running at this point, and I was self-aware enough to know that I needed to understand more. Even though I had generated revenue and a healthy income, from the age of 15, I expected I needed something extra to build something more permanent.

3. I took full advantage of all experiences offered to me. From the early days in the BiG Challenge with Gabe through to my time at university, I made sure I engaged fully in every opportunity. I won National Young Freelancer of the Year from IPSE, won an inspirational student award for Enterprise and Entrepreneurship, and Ambassador of the Year for Youth Employment UK. I was around to take advantage of these opportunities and worked hard to ensure I came out with the awards. I pushed myself forward, which, if you remember my damaged confidence, took an immense amount of resilience.

4. I continue to pursue what is important to me. I am building my profile as a public speaker on mental health issues and LGBTQ+ rights. I speak about these in my blog and produce articles and have radio slots on these issues too. Building up my profile and ensuring that being authentic helps differentiate me in a competitive market. I do a lot that doesn't get paid for because it means when a client comes along, and they want to hire me, they can see that they are getting a good person.

5. Find your support team. Remember how much support I received from my form tutor? Then, how much guidance I received from David and Pete, my mentors who chose to take a real interest in my success, and I chose to listen and be willing to be guided.

Takeaways

- Become self-aware, and do a SWOT analysis for your career choice. Being an entrepreneur is the right choice for me; is it for you?
- Use the SWOT as a guide to making better decisions. If your instincts tell you that being an entrepreneur and working for yourself is for you, pursue it. Use what you have learned from the analysis to make better choices.
- Setting up a business worked for me because I followed a passion. I believe the same would be true for you.

PART 2

Getting Started

CHAPTER 3

Pathways to Entrepreneurship

In this section, learn how to find your passion or spot a gap, both are great ways to become an entrepreneur.

There are two paths that entrepreneurs often take when choosing to start a business. The first, which is a worthy approach, is to see a need in the market and build a business plan. Another way of seeing this is to notice the significant problems in the world and set about solving them while making money at the same time. It is the truest win–win scenario, as the world has something it needs, and an entrepreneur is independently wealthy.

Choosing path one, to be the solver of market problems, you need to be sure you have seen the solution that (a) will work and (b) will make money while it works. These innovations are not rare, but they are often driven by someone who is either talented or visionary and who can find people to fund them while they build what they imagined.

Path two, well, this was my path. You find something that you love, and you make this into your job. Love to write? Set up a copywriting business. Love to design? Set up a design business. It is something that you enjoy, and you can sell this service to someone else.

While I admire those who take the first path, I know most about my path. My path was to follow one of my loves and make money from it. So, let's dive deep into this approach to entrepreneurship.

Identify Your Passion

I have always loved technology and am still obsessed with trying new devices. I would follow the tech news, and I would teach myself how to make the most of technology by watching YouTube videos. Such was my interest that friends and family would come to me to solve their tech problems, as I knew about devices and how to fix them, well, most of the time. In reality, I decided what I didn't know I would learn, and I learned quickly. As I was interested and passionate, I was happy to put in this work because it didn't feel like work.

Confucius said, "Choose a job you love, and you will never have to work a day."

It is powerful wisdom and is easier to achieve than it is to say. Yet, starting my business doing something I was doing as a hobby got me there. I was fortunate, though, in two different ways. One, I was clear on what I loved to do and had pinpointed a passion early. It is not always so simple to find out what you love doing, and certainly harder still to shape this into a viable business. Second, I started my business at a young age, while I was still living with my parents. I had few financial responsibilities, so I could survive the early days when my passion didn't pay me anything.

Let's break this problem down step by step. How can you identify your passion?

Like me, your truest passion probably emerged when you were a child. It was the time when you were free to do whatever you enjoyed most, without the daily pressures of adult life. What did you find yourself doing when time stopped as you found yourself completely lost in an activity? Were you building something in Lego or putting together models of planes? Were you doing science experiments? Did you enjoy looking after people or running around outside, spending time in nature? Whatever brought you joy as a child is likely the passion you can pursue in your work.

You then need to forget the practicalities for a while. Sure, you need money, and you might need to do a side hustle while you build up your business. However, the best way to follow your passions from childhood is to think like a child. You need to imagine if money were no object what would you do? What would you choose to do even if you weren't paid to do it? By asking these questions and eliminating money from the decision, you get closer to your passion. It might feel scary, and this is a good thing. Fear, when we think about opportunities in our life, is a barometer for what we care about. If we are afraid, it is because we don't want to lose this or fail at it. Walk toward this fear.

You can also tell a lot about your passions by looking at the people you respect and why you respect them. Who are your professional heroes? It is likely they represent something you value deep inside and so sit close to your passions.

When I started to expand my IT support services into web design, I had no portfolio or experience to help me to be spotted in a crowded market. So, I did something that people might feel is crazy. I did some work for free. I reached out to small businesses and looked for new businesses, like restaurants, that were opening in my area and contacted them. You can imagine their surprise when I offered to create their website for free, most believing it was too good to be true.

While working for free like this doesn't sound like good business sense, I was earning something from these interactions. I was rapidly building up a portfolio that I could use to win paid work. I have five websites that the customers were happy with and who offered me testimonials about my work. As I was passionate, working days to get the site right, I was able to publish these projects in a week. I was able to use free website builders like Wix and WordPress, which were perfect for small businesses, and the five projects I completed got me started.

Fortunately, you don't have to work for free in today's world of freelancers and the gig economy. Sites like Fiverr and Upwork allow you to bid for work and build a portfolio while earning money. You do need to accept, even on these sites, that you will start by earning a low amount until you build your rating and have evidence of your abilities.

If you are working on your passion, none of this work will feel like work. When you start getting paid, you will feel a sense of surprise and pride that someone will pay you for what you love doing.

Seeing a Problem That Needed Solving

While the start of my time as an entrepreneur was focused on my passion, my business developed because I saw a gap in offering influencer marketing at the start of the era of YouTubers, who were becoming increasingly popular. I noticed that there was an opportunity to create a list of influencer contacts and so got in touch with vloggers and contacted a host of brands. I pitched a campaign to vloggers and handled everything on behalf of the brand. Essentially, I became an intermediary communicating between the vlogger and the client and ensuring the campaigns ran smoothly for both parties.

I began this business when brands knew they wanted to make the most of influencer marketing and had no idea how to go about it. I knew how to do it, and so solved a problem for them. It was a profitable business because I leveraged my superior knowledge and used the idea of surprising and delighting in building excellent relationships. I took the lessons from my computer business when working with clients and knew how to build a positive reputation.

Vloggers themselves are a great example of an individual spotting an opportunity and leveraging it. Yet, before you set about becoming a social media influencer, you need to remember the first point I made. You may think making and watching videos on YouTube and earning your fame and fortune is a brilliant extension of your hobby, and so do millions of others. While at the start, in about 2013/4, you might have gotten away with vapid content with little point or value, now the competition is huge. Those vloggers making their money have genuine talent, and I can tell you that the influencers I work with have developed the skills necessary to be highly competitive in this market.

Have a look at where Zoella (Zoe Sugg) started her influencer career. She began by making make-up tutorials. She started with a small audience, as most influencers do, and persevered until her videos became popular. She now has her range of beauty products and two best-selling novels and has featured in an ad campaign for YouTube itself. Think of the resilience Zoe Sugg showed to keep going when no one was watching and then the vision to know she needed to expand her career beyond YouTube to increase her influence. She may have started doing something she loved, and she spotted opportunities to expand in those gaps in the market that needed a solution.

Takeaways

- Doing what you love as an entrepreneur guarantees you will never work a day in your life.

- You need to start small and build your reputation, charging a reasonable amount until you have a portfolio to evidence your ability.
- Keep a look out for the problem that needs solving, as even if you start with a passion, you should be looking for the next opportunity.

CHAPTER 4

Planning

In this section, learn how to get started the right way, remembering to learn as you go along.

Right, time to be honest. I am about to share with you what you should do rather than what I did do. Most great businesses are built because there is a solid and detailed plan in place, which answers all the questions needing answering before the business is started. As I began mending my friends and family's computers, I didn't have a plan. I learned as I went along and went through some trial and error to work out the best way forward. I am never going to suggest you stop learning, as even the best-laid plans go wrong, and you need to learn from why they didn't go the way you hoped. However, I am going to suggest that you write a great business plan and avoid all those preventable mistakes, saving yourself much heartache.

Ask the Right Questions

Before you get started with your business idea, sit down and answer the key questions that form the basis of a great plan.

1. **What is the need you are satisfying?**
   What you offer must fulfill a need that exists in the market. While some ingenious people can generate desire in a market, take Steve Jobs as an example, it is rare. It is best to start a business where there is a genuine demand for your product or services. I started mending computers because most people I knew were genuinely baffled why their computer sometimes stopped working or didn't do what it was meant to. I could drop by and solve this for them, and they would pay me. This scenario offers the perfect seed for a business idea.

2. **How will you satisfy the need?**

The trick of an entrepreneur is to know how to satisfy the needs of the market before someone else. Sometimes it is easy. My computer isn't working, and I work out how to make it work. Imagine the first person who thought that there needed to be a way of meeting face to face without all having to travel to the same place. It took someone with great imagination to envision and innovate video conferencing.

Creativity is one of the greatest qualities of an entrepreneur. Imagination isn't always about painting pictures or writing novels; sometimes, it is about coming up with the best solution to a problem.

3. **How are you different?**

Unless you are very lucky, you are going to be entering a market where you have lots of competitors. There are likely others who are trying to satisfy the same need, and yours needs to be different enough that they choose you. This unique selling point, aka USP, will differentiate you from your competitors. If you don't know what that is, your customers won't either.

4. **Who needs to be involved with you in your business?**

I have always been a solo entrepreneur. I have worked for myself and not employed others. However, this does not mean I have worked alone. I have hired other freelancers to help me deliver contracts, and I have coordinated between clients, acting as the intermediary. Therefore, there are key stakeholders in my business, which I identified and then ensured I managed this relationship.

You might need to onboard staff, form a management team, and bring on some advisors. Who are these people who will help you turn your business into a success?

5. **How big is the market you are entering?**

The more niche your idea, the smaller the market. The more mainstream your idea, the more competitors there will be and the smaller your share of the market. You are looking for an idea that means there is a big enough share of the market for you and that your offer is attractive enough to make a profit. It is difficult, and sometimes you have to get started to learn more about the market.

6. **Who is your target customer?**

You can't possibly serve the needs of everyone, and if you try, you will probably end up pleasing nobody. Even the major supermarkets, around for a long time, know that they won't be the go-to shop for everybody. They each have an idea of a target customer, broken down by demographics such as gender, age, social position, job, and so on. All the products they choose and the advertising they undertake will be influenced by this understanding.

Think about Zoe Sugg again. She knew she was speaking to girls of her age who liked make-up and beauty products. She stuck to this and made sure all her content was appealing to her most likely market. She might not have known she was doing this when she started, and I suspect she learned to home this message as she went along. You will probably have to do the same.

7. **How will you get people to know about your business?**

It's all well and good to have a brilliant idea for a business, but if no one knows about it, you are never going to be successful. Marketing and promotional strategies are essential to being successful. I might have started my IT business with friends and family, but I grew because of word of mouth. My website design service started with five businesses, all of which offered me positive testimonials that I put on my own website. It is here that knowing your target market is essential, as you need to understand where they go looking when they are looking to satisfy that need you spotted.

8. **How will you make money?**

The economics of your business is the most important part of your success. While I love making my clients happy, I also want to be financially independent. Therefore, being aware of pricing, costs, margins, and expenses is essential.

Getting the right price is part science and part art. You can do the math and work out how much it costs to give your service or make your product, and then add a little on top as profit. The problem comes when someone else can do it cheaper than you or you are priced at the same as everyone else. If you think being the one to offer the lowest price is the right option, think about how many times you have judged the lowest price as being the worst quality. Here lies the complexity!

You will also need money to get started. Even in my business competition while still at school, I needed £25 from the competition organizers to buy materials to make our product. Who is going to give you the initial funds to help you launch your business idea? If you need to get a loan or an investor, you then need to play with the figures to work out when you will break even.

But What If Your Assumptions Are Wrong?

When answering all these questions, you will make a lot of assumptions. You will guess who would like your product or service. You will guess how many you can sell. You will guess how much it takes to provide the service and product and how many customers you can provide to in the time given.

There is a saying: when you assume you make an ASS of U and ME.

The only thing that matters when building a business is that you achieve product/market fit. What does this mean? Well, you need to be sure that your idea does satisfy the needs of your target audience. There are lots to test here. First, is it the right idea? Second, is it the right market? And third, does my market have the money to buy the solution I have for their needs?

If you get any of these assumptions wrong, you don't have product/market fit, and you don't have a successful idea.

Consequently, you need to test your assumption and find out before you waste a lot of money failing. I have been fortunate that most of my businesses or services have low start-up costs, and I could learn quickly if I was wrong. It would have taken me only a few months of continual rejections from clients of my influencer marketing service before I realized I had gotten it wrong.

Most other businesses do not benefit from this luxury and so need to set up surveys and tests to find out before expending too much capital.

There are masses of tools out there to help you find out if your idea works or not. You can build a minimal viable product (the cheapest version of your idea that actually works) and get the people you think might like it to try it out.

Unfortunately, Kevin Costner's "Build it, and he will come" quote has left many people disappointed. It is always best to use market research tools to make sure they will come when you properly develop your product or service.

Writing Your Business Plan

It is likely that you will need a business plan before you will get serious funding from a bank or investor. If you are happy with starting small and creating a "gig" business where there is no need for investment, you can probably self-fund and so do not need to formally write down your plan. If you want to build a business that will quickly allow you to fund your life, you will need to commit to writing the answers to all those questions in a formalized way.

A business plan offers those who might fund the business details of your idea, the market you have identified, how you will operate, and how you will make money. The simple question this plan is answering is: why will this business succeed when most others fail?

And here is a fact to consider right here, right now. Twenty percent of startups fail in the first year. This figure rises to 60 percent by the end of the third year.

While this is not a fact intended to put you off, it is a reality check. Your investors will know this and will be looking for why your business will beat the odds. What thinking have you done when answering all those questions and testing out your ideas, which means you have guaranteed your success?

There are a huge number of templates on the Internet that you can use to shape your ideas.

Instead of regurgitating the different sections, you need to write, let's instead focus on what success looks like.

First, your business plan needs to be concise. Imagine your investor sees a lot of these plans and has limited time to spare to understand your idea. Therefore, you need to focus only on what your reader needs to know, cutting out the waffle and ensuring you don't bury the lead. In short, you need to start with a focused description of your idea and quickly explain why it will work.

Second, put relevant details in an appendix. So, when you write your plan, keep each section brief but provide links to files that show your research, the CVs of all those involved, tech specs if appropriate, as well as your detailed financial forecasts.

Third, be realistic. There is no point in being overly optimistic or hyping up the language. The person reading your plan will suspect you are trying too hard, and it will work against you. Therefore, keep everything believable and make sure you seed credibility with your reader.

Fourth, the financial section of your business plan will make or break your idea. You need to know your stuff and have broken down the figures appropriately. Approaching an independent financial advisor that is authorized and regulated by the Securities and Exchange Commission (SEC) in the United States and the Financial Conduct Authority (FCA) in the United Kingdom is advisable. These advisors can help you get the finances right and help you forecast sensibly, and so be a viable business opportunity.

Finally, and most importantly, make your plan professional. There should be no spelling errors, it should have a cover and a contents page, make sure there is an executive summary that gives a top-level sell of your idea, and, where possible, use charts to illustrate numbers.

Here's a top tip. Spend a little money and get a copywriter to write it for you or a professional proofreader to scan through your work. Investing a little here could make you a ton of money later on.

And SWOT Again

Your business plan will stand out if you include a SWOT analysis. It makes sense that you want someone to know your strengths and the opportunities that exist for you. Yet, it might feel counterintuitive to include your weaknesses and threats. However, denying that these factors exist is dangerous and will worry your reader. There is power in acknowledging those barriers to success because you can say how you are going to mitigate them too.

Remember, if you don't identify the downsides to your idea, the investor or bank manager will. If they cannot see where you have addressed their worries in your plan, they will reject your idea. Consequently, the most powerful section of this business plan could be this SWOT analysis, where you show you have thought of everything.

Takeaways

- Know your idea inside out.
- Write the ideas for your business into a clear and professional plan.
- Seek professional advice and help to ensure your business plan is the best it can be.

CHAPTER 5

Getting to Know Your Customers

In this section, knowing the people who are going to part with their money will help you surprise and delight them. It is the only way to ensure they come back!

There are two ways that knowing your customers helps. First, if you are a service business, as I am, it helps you build relationships. However, even in a business where you will never meet your customers in person, they still need to feel known by you.

Second, it helps to know your customers because you will know enough to be able to do well enough to encourage them to come back. What you will learn quickly is that winning a new customer is hard. It is really, really hard. Therefore, if you get a new customer, you need to do what you can to increase their lifetime value. What does this mean? Well, it costs you money in advertising and sales to win a customer, and you need them to earn that money back and more. So, every time you get a returning customer, and they keep coming back, their lifetime value to you increases. Ultimately, you want people to be loyal to you for as long as you are in business. The only way to gain this loyalty is by knowing what they need and to keep knowing their needs even when the world changes.

When You Start Out as a Lone Entrepreneur

There is a difference here between what you do when you are working in a larger organization and when you are an entrepreneur looking to start your business. When I started, I used my instinct and understanding of the direct world around me to make decisions. I approached friends and family first, and then when looking to set up websites, approached new businesses that were probably on a limited budget. I can make these seem like clever and analytical decisions made after much research, or I can be honest and say I had a hunch these would be good options.

I also found out, during my years in business, that customers will change over time, and it is important to be agile. When I started my business with IT support, my customers were small business owners and start-ups with less than five staff who needed occasional tech support. These businesses didn't have a huge budget to spend on one of my more established competitors, so they reached out to me. They needed someone to set up new devices or resolve broadband and virus issues, and maybe some support setting up security systems. My home IT support was mostly made up of retired people from wealthier households who were looking to stay connected through technology.

Whether I found these early markets or they were the ones that approached me, I learned quickly that is where the demand was and made sure I kept looking in these places.

Later, when my business evolved to be more about digital marketing services, mostly web design to begin with, I was mostly working for startups with a modest budget. I had learned from my early experiences that these were the ones looking for a brilliant experience for a cheaper price, and so this is where I positioned myself. It has helped me build my portfolio, which then helps me win new customers.

It sounds like I had worked out my customers completely and was on a roll. However, there is a downside to the approach I took. I expanded from website building to social media and copywriting. I was getting a lot of work but I was earning little money. I was having to work hard for a relatively low per-hour income. So, my client base was growing but I was earning low pay.

There comes a tipping point when your portfolio and testimonials allow you to be more confident in whom you can target. I have started to introduce more premium pricing and aim my services at more established markets. The irony is that these bigger companies often pay me more and expect much less from me. My early clients were demanding and often sucked more time than they had originally indicated. These larger clients understood how to give a brief and what was expected as part of the agreement when beginning working for me. It allowed me to work less and earn more.

I am not suggesting you skip the first steps I took. I am exemplifying how your clients will evolve with you, and you need to be mindful of the moment you should be targeting different groups. Since becoming established as a founder of a digital agency, I have been able to establish a client base of established small- to medium-sized enterprises (SMEs) and small brands. As my business and reputation grow, so will the quality of my clients.

My focus, digital marketing, lends itself better to the quality of clients over a number of customers. Your business idea might work better by hiring people to take on the work and allow you to leverage your reputation that way. You have to decide what your customers need from you and the best way to grow your business. More on this later!

When You Are Bigger and More Established

There comes a time when you switch from being a person working for themselves to a person owning a business. You might not know when the switch happens. One day you are gigging and winning customers ad hoc, the next minute, you are working for an established list of clients and have registered yourself as a company.

When you are the founder of a company, you will want to know your customers better. You may need to write a business plan at some point or a deck for an investor, and you will be expected to know who you are targeting. As much as you would like to think everyone in the world is a potential customer, this is far from the truth.

There are three terms to help you here. There is TAM, SAM, and SOM.

If you live in a world of make-believe, you might write down your TAM. This is the Total Addressable Market. For me, well, this would be the whole world that owns a computer. A solid 2 billion people are waiting to be served by my digital agency.

Unrealistic? Oh yes.

SAM means Serviceable Addressable Market. This means what part of this total market can I realistically hope to service? It is probably best for me to believe that I am aiming my services at those in the United Kingdom.

Still, the whole of the United Kingdom is not going to be interested in my digital services—unfortunately.

SOM means Serviceable Obtainable Market. What does this mean? Well, what part of the market do I have a realistic chance of obtaining? Remember when I started out, I aimed at start-ups and retired people who wanted help but didn't want to pay a lot. This was the market obtainable to me. Now, I am targeting SMEs and small brands who are looking to build a relationship with a small digital agency. It makes up less than 1 percent of the companies in the United Kingdom.

Being successful in your business means knowing which part of the market you have a chance of obtaining and targeting your messaging to them.

So, what do you need to know about your customers?

1. Who are they? What is the gender, age, and occupation of your perfect market? What industry do they work in, and what is the size of the business?

2. What do they do? Make sure you know how they spend their day. It means understanding their work and appreciating what they like to do in their spare time. You need to know what they are trying to achieve and, more importantly, what might be blocking them from doing it. The pain points they face are your opportunities!

3. Why do they buy? You need to understand what motivates them toward a buying decision. Running a business is sometimes about understanding the psychology of your customer.

4. When do they buy it? There is a time of day, week, month, or season when your customer is more likely to buy. Being available to them at these times increases your chance of success. If you sell Christmas cards, for instance, it is a good idea to up your marketing around November time.

5. How do they buy? Some customers like to see you in person, while others want to deal with the transaction over the Internet. Some like to pay in cash, even now, while others will pay by a card or Internet payment systems.

6. How much money do they have to spend? Unless you are selling one of life's essentials or providing a service that a person cannot

live without, you are going to need a customer to have disposable income. How much money do they have to spare for you? If there is little money in your customer's pockets, you might struggle to get your business off the ground.

7. What makes your customer feel good when they are buying? There are a lot of people who only buy when they feel they are making an ethical decision. Other people get a buzz out of buying because of the experience offered by the company. I once bought a book because I got a free coaching session with the author who wrote it. It made me happy, and I bought the book.

8. What do your customers expect from you? My early customers expected me to be available time and again to serve their needs. My current customers expect me to complete their briefs. Meeting expectations is core to building a loyal customer base, and exceeding expectations get you a positive testimonial.

9. What do your customers think about you? You need to keep asking people for reviews and testimonials. This isn't a way to stroke your ego. Listening to your customer helps you learn what you need to do better and what you are doing right and should do more in the future.

10. What do your customers think about your competitors? Again, constantly learning is key to understanding how to keep your customers. Finding out what people love about your competitors helps you do this too. If you can puzzle out the gap in their approach, there lies an opportunity to be better than them.

How to Segment and Research Your Market

You can do what I did and use a hunch to find your market. A hunch works if you are open-minded and ready to accept that your hunch is wrong. A better way to express this is that I had a theory of what might work and I tested it out. If the test failed, as it sometimes did, I adapted my theory. In other words, I put in place some practical research to see who would be interested in working for me.

Now I run a digital agency, market segmentation is a big part of the success of my work. I need to be able to understand what people need from me and then provide that. Therefore, to find the answers to all the questions from the previous section, I would need to do my research and analyze the results.

Research begins by defining your market using your best understanding. Looking at competitors is a great way of understanding the market, if you are unclear yourself. Once you have an idea of who might be interested, do a SWOT analysis for that market sector.

If you are happy that these are the people for you, then look into what they are like generally. What behaviors are common in these people? What do they like? What trends do they follow? Imagine if your market was playground mums, there is a whole lot of shared behavior and preferences there to find out.

Once you have some understanding of the audience, create a buyer persona. It is even a good idea to give this persona a name and to think about them whenever you are putting an idea together for your business. If Jenny, mother of Ollie (3) and Ella (1), doesn't like your idea for young mums, then it is possibly not the way you should go. In other words, it helps you stay on track and make sensible decisions because you can test it against your persona.

It is possible to have more than one persona. It is a good idea to make up people for each of the markets you are looking to target and to think of them when you are making choices.

Whatever choices you make when writing these personas, you need to test them out all the time. Having a theory is good; constantly working out if the theory holds true is better. You will find over time, with the evidence you collect, your personas will evolve, and you will get better and better at targeting the customers for your business. You just need to be open to learning.

Takeaways

- Know that you cannot work with everybody.
- Turn your hunches into theories and keep on questioning.
- Keep your customers, as winning new customers is hard!

CHAPTER 6

Make a Backup Plan

In this section, you need to understand how hard it is to get started and the reality of what life might be like.

When you write a book after you have built your business, it is easy to give the impression that it is easy to be an entrepreneur. It isn't. When I first started out, I had very few customers and was making little money. I certainly wasn't earning enough to pay my way in life.

Therefore, of all the advice I have given you about getting started, this is my most important: have a backup plan.

My story of working while building my business started when I was 15. I am a young entrepreneur, remember, and my IT support business was started when I was still at school. Therefore, there are some realities I didn't have to face. I was living with my parents and so did not face huge monthly bills. I liked to pay my way, and my parents were always there to be my backup plan. In this way, my story might be different from yours.

If you are older and starting out, you may need to work full-time while you are building your business. As I said, at the age of 16 I worked for a large electrical retailer while building my business. It started as a Christmas job and then I was offered a paid position as a technical support advisor soon after I started. I was now setting up people's laptops for a huge company. This was something that got in the way of my business but it was also a valuable learning experience, as I found out a lot about scaling up IT support.

It was depressing working this way. I was sent to a quiet back office and given 100 laptops to set up each shift. It was lonely and laborious, and most days, mundane. It helped me hone my IT skills and it taught me that I really wanted to run my business. It also made me realize that IT support wasn't my passion. It was not the business I wanted to build—hence I switched to something more creative and started with my digital agency.

However, the truth is that I needed that job to earn enough to live. I had to keep going to work while I built up my business, as I needed to supplement my income. As well as working at this large retailer I have worked as a receptionist at a local swimming pool and gym, packed manufacturing tools, and worked in a local supermarket.

When you start your business, it will likely need to be a side hustle. Quitting everything to get started is a mistake. You need to build up your business to a point it sustains you and then you can quit your day job. While I struggled to get over the fact I needed the job, as I had been earning money from my business from a young age, I really needed to swallow my pride. The character you show by taking on the extra work while you build your reputation and client base is an essential part of being an entrepreneur. You do what it takes—and this sometimes means having a backup plan.

Finding the Right Balance

So, you are likely going to be working full-time while you start your business. This is tough. You are going to need to find a way of balancing your freelance gigs with your full-time job. It is likely, if you are not careful, going to take a toll on your mental and physical energy and steal a lot of your free time.

Here are some essential tips to make sure you are getting the balance right:

1. If the gigs you are doing are things you enjoy, then you are likely not going to feel like you are working. If you like to write, then getting paid to write is a bonus. Making sure your freelance work is a passion makes it easier to balance the tasks with your full-time work.

2. Make sure you are realistic about the clients you can take on and the timelines you can offer. When doing freelance gigs, your biggest route to success comes from managing the expectations of your clients. Take on only what you can manage and be clear to them when you deliver and then deliver on time!

3. Prioritize the full-time job. As much as you might see the full-time job as a means to an end—as a way of helping you earn while you

build your business—your boss won't see it this way. If your freelance business isn't paying enough to cover your rent and food, then you need that full-time job. Keep the two separate and make sure you keep your responsibilities to the work that is paying your way.

4. Realize that it takes a lot of time to onboard a client, and this is time you are not being paid for. When you are starting a business, you will exchange a lot of messages with new clients and this will take your available time. Be realistic, therefore, about how many of these conversations you can manage and learn from each experience, streamlining how you bring your gig clients on board.

5. Choose clients in different time zones. Working with people who are at a different time to you can be really useful. If you are working 9 to 5 on your full-time job, then working with someone who is five or six hours behind or ahead means you can do this when you are not working. Working with the United States, for instance, means most of my communication can happen with them between 5 and 9 pm.

6. Decide how much you need to earn on a regular basis to allow yourself to give up your job. If you set yourself a target and work toward this, it can keep you going through the tough days. You know that the hard work you are putting in now won't last forever.

The core thing to remember when starting out is to be realistic. You cannot manage a full-time workload and a full-time freelancing client list. You will let someone down. Therefore, build your freelance client work slowly, learn what it takes to be successful, and be transparent with these customers about what it is possible for you to offer.

Takeaways

- You may need to work full-time while you build your business.
- Prioritize the work that pays your bills, even when you don't want to.
- Be open and transparent about what is realistic for you to achieve in the early days of your business.

PART 3

Growing Your Business

CHAPTER 7

Using Social Media

In this section, Learn why social media is arguably the most important tool you can access in today's world, how you can use it to create a following, and also for retention and business growth.

Choose Your Platforms Wisely

It's easy to lose yourself in searching for the social platforms, which are the right ones for your business, and you. As a general rule, it is preferable to go to the social media space where your target audience spends most of its time, but you will need to do some solid probing to find it. I usually recommend that my clients start by focusing on two platforms, and get them right before moving on to sign up for others. It isn't advisable to spread yourself too thin as a new business and remember that even if you are established, maintaining an active social media presence can be exhausting.

Facebook's user base has a significant number of followers across every age group. The latest statistics show that the monthly active users on this platform are nearly 2.85 billion. Making it an excellent place to start for most brands, to increase awareness, or generate leads. On the other hand, if you want to expand your network of influencers and professionals, then Twitter and LinkedIn are likely to be the top options. In contrast, TikTok and Instagram are good choices if you want to appeal to younger audiences.

Whichever channels you choose I can't recommend highly enough that you reveal your personality, when you post and interact with other users. There is nothing more off-putting than an overly corporate social media page! I have worked with lots of different businesses, along with household names. The clients who have been too afraid to open up, and have fun on their social media channels, tend to be the ones I have had to let go. Since however hard you try you will never gain a lot if all you do is sell, sell, sell.

You only have to look at the posts which get the most likes and comments, to see that customers much prefer to be entertained. They also love to see who is behind the brand they are buying from. For that reason, it is a good idea to show them lots of behind-the-scenes footage and make a decision now to get in front of the camera, if you fully intend to make social media work for you. A live video should be an important part of your marketing mix. You could live stream brand events, interviews, and so on. Trust me, it's a great way to increase your audience engagement ratio.

Storytelling for Successful Marketing

It's also important to remember that the way you portray your brand has a huge impact on how people feel about it. Prominent businesses have resorted to using storytelling for the success they have achieved in their brand marketing. As this helps to develop an emotional connection between a target audience, and the brand. The medium through which the story is communicated is equally important. Social media is again a highly effective platform for this.

Some of my favorite examples of the brands effectively using social media in this way include Ryanair and Aldi in the United Kingdom. Also, internationally, KFC and Duolingo. In marketing, you need to be bold, brave, and unafraid to take risks. These companies are definitely leading the way when it comes to this.

Ryanair wasn't afraid to be controversial on Twitter, raising awareness of social issues, and making fun of its competitors. Holding people in the public eye, and the government to account. Using, for example, the party gate scandal in Downing Street during the covid pandemic. Making the tweets fun, entertaining, and occasionally rude. This led to wide mainstream media coverage and comments which referred to the tweets as unprofessional and inappropriate. None of this stopped the marketing team from continuing to retell and develop the stories they had chosen which were already in the public domain.

Ryanair's tweets could never be described as boring, and despite the company being rated as the "worst airline" for seven years in a row by

Which magazine, its customer numbers have grown. Admittedly a low fares policy does seem to appeal, but every time one of its controversial tweets became viral it proved to be another advertisement for the airline.

Aldi has also dominated the Internet with its Twitter campaign to Free Cuthbert which went viral after Marks & Spencer took legal action for an alleged infringement of its intellectual property rights. When Aldi made a cake similar to its Colin the Caterpillar, the marketing team used this as an opportunity to attract massive interest in #FreeCuthbert, and what was happening in the dispute. A case study concluded that Aldi's campaigns increased sales per store by more than 100 percent over three years. The campaign was aimed at millennials and Gen Z who grew up seeing feuds like this, but it is wise to be cautious. This strategy won't necessarily appeal to every audience, or be viable for every business to pursue.

While KFC in the UK and Ireland gained more than 650,000 new buyers because of a campaign based on how no one liked their fries. Using a business problem to improve the product they offered, and leveraging the change to create a brilliant marketing campaign. Again, there wasn't a sales pitch involved, or landing page where those who engaged with the posts were steered toward, but it still proved to be a highly successful move.

Duolingo on TikTok featured Duo the Owl, ignoring what its audience's initial perception of a large green owl might be. Making people laugh instead. At the same time as providing a face for its brand that was quirky, and playful. Not easily forgotten. Catching the attention of NBC News, Insider, and Rolling Stone magazine. This was again about entertainment, not overt sales.

Knowing Which Channels to Use

Choosing the social media that is right for you largely depends on your business niche. I have already mentioned that Facebook is the best if you want to increase brand awareness or generate leads. On the other hand, if you are looking to expand your network of influencers and professionals, then Twitter and LinkedIn may well be the top options. While TikTok and Instagram are likely to appeal to younger demographics.

When considering which channels to use, think about it sensibly! For instance, if you're selling retirement homes, it'll be safe to forgo Snapchat where only 3.7 percent of users are over 50. Here is a little more information about the main platforms you can choose from.

Facebook

Facebook currently attracts 2.89 billion monthly users, more than any other social platform. A high concentration of its audience belongs to Millennials, Gen X-ers, and Baby Boomers. In the last three months, a whopping 91 percent of Baby Boomers, 88 percent of Millennials, and 83 percent of Gen X-ers have visited Facebook.

On top of that, Gen X and Baby Boomers rank Facebook as their favorite social media app, and most visited one. So, if you are looking to target older demographics with social media marketing, Facebook is your best bet.

That said, engagement drops significantly for Gen Z audiences. Just 12 percent of Gen Z-ers say they use Facebook more than any other platform, and only 55 percent have visited Facebook in the past three months.

TikTok

TikTok is known as the platform for Gen Z, and the data confirms it. In fact, over half of Gen Z consumers are on TikTok. Plus, Gen Z-ers say TikTok is the platform they use the most. Pulling ahead of Instagram, Snapchat, and YouTube.

It doesn't stop there! TikTok is also picking up steam with other demographics. In 2021 36 percent of TikTok users were between 35 and 54 years old, a 10 percent increase from the year before. Even so, usage amongst Baby Boomers is still low, with only seven percent visiting the app in the last three months.

It's also worth mentioning that TikTok has the highest engagement rate out of any other social platform, averaging 10.85 minutes per session. In short, TikTok's snackable content is addictive for a variety of age groups.

YouTube

YouTube has a user base of more than 2 billion people, and receives over 34 billion monthly visits, according to data pulled from SimilarWeb.

YouTube is popular with Gen Z, millennial, and Gen X audiences. Almost in equal measure. In the last three months, 83 percent of millennials have visited it, followed by 81 percent of Gen Z, and 79 percent of Gen X. For Baby Boomers, YouTube is their second favorite social media app, just behind Facebook.

YouTube is also a top favorite among video marketers. In fact, more than a quarter of them planned to invest in it than any other platform in 2022, according to HubSpot's Video Marketing Report. In addition, video marketers ranked YouTube as the second-best platform for return on investment (ROI).

Instagram

According to SimilarWeb, the Instagram app has over 78 million monthly active users, making it one of the most popular apps today.

Although Gen Z visits TikTok the most, they rank Instagram as their favorite social media app. As do millennials.

Instagram is also holding steady with older audiences. In the last three months, 55 percent of Gen X-ers have visited Instagram, followed by more than a quarter (27%) of Baby Boomers. However, if you're looking to target these audiences specifically, Facebook or YouTube could be the better option.

On the marketing side, more than half of video marketers rank Instagram as the best platform for ROI, engagement, and lead generation. If you are looking to dive further into it, Instagram is an attractive option.

LinkedIn

LinkedIn is great if you're selling B2B, and looking to connect with key decision makers. Not all of my clients are on this platform, as many of them are B2C businesses, but for a business owner or young professional, it is important to have a LinkedIn presence. Here are a few good reasons why:

1. It can help you increase your web traffic, so get known. Your name will show up on Google searches, and you can use the features on

the platform to increase your search engine rankings. When current and potential clients may be looking for a solution to their problems.

2. It can create a much better first impression. So, make sure you introduce your business properly, tell the story of your brand, showcase your talents, and share helpful insights. This will help you to stand out from your competitors.

3. It can create a strong network for your business. After all, that's what LinkedIn is about! Also help you build a reputation as an expert, or the "go to" person in your field. Your audience should be more confident about approaching you when they see your connections. Plus, any endorsements you have received for your skills, and references.

4. It can help you attract new talent as your business grows. Top candidates usually expect a comparable employer to have a great LinkedIn presence. College students looking to get a foot on the career ladder can also find it a helpful site.

5. LinkedIn can make you use your imagination. When you have a more in-depth look at other businesses and your professional contacts. Also, see what is trending in or around your field of expertise. This can give you a lot of ideas for developing your own business.

6. Don't get left behind! The more your business grows and the busier you get; it can be easy to lose sight of what is happening in your sector or comparable businesses. For example, the current technology being used, common problems, and so on. It isn't enough to just have a LinkedIn account. You need to use it and take full advantage of its features.

Continue to Share Your Story

I go into schools, colleges, and universities to run workshops and share my story. I always encourage the young people I am speaking to (if they're sixteen or over) to join LinkedIn. Since this is the place where I have found a number of lucrative opportunities, met clients, and built my profile as a digital expert. In recent years, I started to use my LinkedIn profile as a blog. Taking advantage of its "write an article" function, to share both my personal and professional stories. Raising awareness of specific topics. I even posted my coming out story on LinkedIn.

Any negative reaction I received from followers and clients to more personal posts showed me that these were not the people I wanted in my network, or I would necessarily be comfortable working with.

However, I still believe that it is vitally important to reveal your personality on LinkedIn, if you feel able to do this. The platform is essentially an online networking event, in which all of us with a LinkedIn account can take part. Imagine how boring it would be if you met someone at an event like this whom you thought had zero personality. Simply because they hadn't revealed anything in their posts or comments which might make you think otherwise. Isn't it highly likely that you would move on, so lose the chance of working with them, and miss the fantastic business opportunities you might otherwise have had?

Organic Versus Paid Advertising

I work mainly in organic social media management, and in the majority of cases, discourage my clients from spending a lot of money on paid advertising. As I strongly believe that working on your organic social media is better in the long run, and much cheaper too.

When you pay for platforms like Facebook, and Instagram, you can have your content shared with specific audiences. These can be targeted by you, and filters used. Using demographics, location, interests, and so on. Cost per click is one of the most common ways of charging for this type of promotion. It is usually done to raise brand awareness, attract new followers, get more leads, or drive conversions.

The other alternative is to adopt a hybrid approach or a mixture of both paid and unpaid promotion. Depending on the type of business you have, how long you have been trading, your budget, and your attitude to risk.

Creating a Following That Will Engage With You

It is very important that you stay in your own lane when you start creating a following. At the outset, I was like a lot of people. I focused on getting a large following, because I felt that this would validate my expertise. In reality, all it did was make me feel negative, an imposter, and caused me a lot of stress. When it is far better to use your social media platforms in a positive way, to shine a light on your business, and the topics you care about. Since this will bring engagement, and followers who will come naturally to you. Instead of you chasing the numbers, because at the end of the day, these don't mean anything by themselves.

Building an engaged audience on social media is where the real-time investment comes in. When you listen to your people, you will have the opportunity to understand their problems, their dreams, what they love, and hate. Getting inside their minds will help you find the right way to engage with them, how you can help them, and create content they will love. Then follow this up, by being there. Every single day! Listening, responding, and sharing content that they want. It is an investment of your time, but something that will pay off with bonuses when you get it right.

To build a real and loyal social media community, you need to be active and only publish content that provides value to the reader. Buying fake followers to boost your numbers is a waste of time and money and can often hurt your reputation. If you are posting five to seven times every week on your channels, you should also only include a maximum of one to two sales posts in these. The rest of the content should add value to your followers, and you should also offer an opinion on trending topics or news stories related to your industry. I have found that it is much better to keep the content mixed. Offering a range of graphic-based posts, videos, and longer-form content.

Commenting and sharing others' posts, becoming an authority on your subject, attending industry events, being yourself, providing information that provokes reactions are just some of the things that help engagement. Even then success is unlikely to come overnight. It takes persistence and dedication which are sometimes hard to justify. So, outsourcing at least some of your social media requirements is definitely worth considering when you can afford to do this.

In the meantime, if you spend ten minutes every day commenting and engaging with others' posts, this will help get your own content seen. Especially on LinkedIn. Stay positive and become involved in some larger conversations. Users of the platforms you are on will start to see you then as an expert. Maybe even a thought leader. Consistency and good content are the King and Queen in this game. Without either of them, the growth of loyal fans will more than likely drop, as quickly as it could have grown.

Something else which helped me get started was to write guest articles for well-known sites and publications. You might like to contact your local newspapers and offer to write opinion columns for them. Once you have gained some experience from this, reach out to national, and international publications. I have been lucky enough to be featured in a huge number of well-respected publications, including Forbes. All of which helped to validate my business expertise and reputation, also to grow an engaged following.

Takeaways

- It isn't necessary to be on every social media platform, only those where you will find your audience.
- The current trend is to be bold, brave, and unafraid to take risks in optimizing your marketing results. However, you need to be careful when doing this. Despite the success it can bring, being controversial is a high-risk strategy that doesn't always work for every audience or platform.
- Maintain an up-to-date LinkedIn account. So that clients, new talent, and other industry professionals receive a good impression of your brand and get to know who you really are.

CHAPTER 8

Networking

In this section, learn to the network by talking to people at events or online, also reach out to professionals and others who have the potential to help your career and business grow.

How I Started Networking

When I started building my network and social contacts, I soon discovered that I needed to be the real me. Not put on an act to impress anyone. I noticed that when I smiled and was authentic, others seemed willing to share their ideas and experiences. I was honest about where I had reached in my career journey. Even though I might not have managed to achieve a lot in their eyes, if anything at the start, I had my interests along with hopes and dreams. I knew what I would love to come next, and those were the things I talked about. I developed long-term relationships with others from doing this, and mutual trust. Helping my career path, and in time, both of our businesses to grow. So that I am able now to help other young entrepreneurs who wish to make a start, in the same way as I did.

Although it was hard sometimes, especially at first, I realize now how rewarding all of this has been. I have met some of my best friends through networking. I discovered too how important it is not to be afraid when reaching out to others. After I had entered the enterprise competition at school for the third time offering IT support, and found out that I had been shortlisted for one of the final awards, I reached out to Chikumo Fiseko. She was one of the winners from the previous year. All I did was send her a message on Twitter to ask if she could help me in any way with my public speaking, also in preparing my presentation for the final. I didn't really expect a reply, so I was thrilled when she offered to meet me for coffee. She said that she could give me some tips from her experience of the competition and review the slide deck I had prepared for the judges.

I can still remember my Dad dropping me off at Starbucks that day, and being nervous before I went inside. Sending a message to Chikumo was a huge step for me to take! It was the first time I had asked anyone for help from my wider network, but sometimes you just have to shoot your shot, and this time it paid off. We clicked, instantly. Chatting for hours, over coffee, and hot chocolate. It was beyond anything I could have imagined back then, and the beginning of a long-lasting friendship. We decided to meet every couple of weeks after that. Since we were both self-employed, we thought it could be a great opportunity to become a sounding board for each other, and that particular branch of Starbucks became our regular haunt.

Just as our friendship has continued to grow over the years so have our businesses, and Chikumo has also become my concert buddy. Even though she relocated from Sheffield to Northern Ireland in 2016, we still try to see each other as often as possible. It is one of those true friendships where we are instantly able to pick up where we left off. Irrespective of how much time has passed.

Whilst it all began because we had similar interests, and I plucked up the courage that day to reach out to her on Twitter.

Networking Doesn't Stop.... So, Carry On!

I met another great friend when I was a volunteer at a local enterprise festival in 2015. Using LinkedIn this time, I connected with a specialist for one of the UK's largest examination boards. She was interested in learning more about my story and wanted to know how she could help. Again, we met for coffee and soon formed another lasting friendship. Ruth Carter is one of the kindest people I know. She has been very supportive when I have needed this, and simply being around her feels like a warm hug. We talked about my journey up to that point, where I would like to go next after I had left the sixth form, how I had started to transition into digital marketing and wanted to use my following to support other young people like myself. The more I talked to her the easier it became.

Ruth was incredibly generous in introducing me to her own network. She arranged for me to go to London for the day, with my expenses paid. So that I could learn more about one of the organizations she felt passionate about: Youth Employment UK. I was invited as her plus one to an event in the Houses of Parliament where I could observe other young people, sharing their stories and experiences with the MPs. I went on to meet Laura-Jane Rawlings, CEO of Youth Employment UK, who asked me if I wanted to join them as a Youth Ambassador and I was thrilled to be given the opportunity.

Ruth was able to secure two work placements for me through her contacts. This was with one of the world's largest theme park operators, Merlin Entertainments. She was working at one of their attractions as a part-time actor. I will be grateful to her forever for this! As those placements helped me learn many of the skills I use today in social media. They also led to other opportunities within the organization, and for me to find my niche. I discovered that I love working with businesses in the hospitality sector. Where you can always find lots of exciting things happening and plenty of opportunities for promotion on their social channels.

Of course, there could have been an element of luck in this. Even so, it is still a prime example of what can happen. Simply by taking one of your first steps in networking, and reaching out to others.

The Positive Effect of Volunteering

After I became an ambassador for Youth Employment UK, I was inspired by the organization's people and work. So much so that my own charity work began, and which remains a key component of my personal values today. Something which has changed my life for the better. Despite not earning an income from volunteering, the contacts I made from being in this role have continued to generate many paid opportunities which I might not otherwise have had.

Laura-Jane Rawlings, the CEO of Youth Employment UK, also helped me gain confidence. When I didn't have enough courage to take the next step and move into the spotlight, to showcase my abilities, and what I could do to help others. I was given the opportunity to speak regularly in the Houses of Parliament, and at high-profile events around the United Kingdom. This enabled me in time to help, and support, a lot of young people from underprivileged backgrounds. Something which I have found very rewarding.

Keep Going! Even When Networking Seems Too Difficult

Unfortunately, an inevitable part of networking is that not everyone you meet will be nice but it's important not to give up. I can safely say now, that all of the positive experiences I have had far outweigh the negative ones.

I started to network at 15 years old. When the contacts I met during the school enterprise competition invited me to their events. I found the thought of going into a crowded room back then, and talking about myself, daunting to say the least. However, the biggest challenge I had to overcome turned out to be my age. I used to get puzzled glances from the guests, followed by looks of surprise, even horror. That I should have been there when I was only a child. I can't say I blame them. It was the same look I used to receive from some of my early clients, who clearly doubted I would be experienced enough to deliver the services I was offering, but no one should discourage someone else like this. You can't judge a book by its cover, and whatever you might be thinking everyone deserves a chance.

I had to work hard at times to show that I deserved a place at the events I attended, and occasionally, it was an uphill battle. I used to hover on the edge of conversations. Hoping that I would get the opportunity to introduce myself, if there was a split-second gap in the conversation, but most of the time I might as well have been invisible. I left my fair share of networking events without gaining anything. Even worse, not talking to a single person. However, the more I persisted the more my confidence grew. I found the courage to interrupt those who would have ignored me earlier, and I was accepted by them once they knew my story.

I eventually realized that it didn't matter where I went, there would always be cliques like this in a community. I specifically avoided some events, because I knew the same faces would be there, and I wouldn't have the opportunity to join in. Nevertheless, if you are faced with this situation, the answer is simple. Try exploring different types of networking events, to find the ones which work for you, and match your values. You are more likely to find yourself attending these regularly.

Trial and error in networking is all part of the process. Until you find what you are looking for, and you will, if you keep going.

Follow Up the Contacts You Make

I always go to an event with a smile and collect business cards from the people I meet. So that I can connect with them on LinkedIn, the following day. Thanking them for their time, I also let them know how I believe we could work together. In my experience, this really does make a difference, and it will help them remember you.

Once the people you meet have your details, inquiries can still pop into your inbox months later. You can't always expect an instant return from attending a networking event, but the more that others see and get to know you, the more likely this will be to happen. In just the same way as social media followers will begin to trust you, the more great content you post for them to read.

Networking can be used to raise your profile, even as an expert in your field, and I can't recommend it highly enough.

Be Prepared to Leave Your Comfort Zone

I used to provide IT tuition to a wonderful and prestigious couple, Sir Hugh Ridley and Lady Ruby Sykes, who lived in a manor house in the Peak District. After I had been working with them for around six months, they invited me to a lavish Christmas party. Even though I was only 16 years old at the time. As you can well imagine, the other guests at the event were rich and influential. The list included a number of business leaders, then there was me. Naturally, I felt out of place, but at the same time incredibly proud. Simply to be there, and again, I had to pluck up the courage to introduce myself to the other guests. Thankfully most of them welcomed me with open arms into their circles, which meant I had a brilliant time.

Looking back now, I have made some wonderful connections in the most unexpected of places. I would like to thank everyone I met at a networking event who has encouraged me, allowed me to share my story, or simply to join in the conversation. You know who you are, but what you may not realize is just how much you helped me.

Takeaways

- An important factor in your professional success will be the connections you make, and the collective power that your network has to help you. So, reach out! Don't be afraid to take the first step in making contact. You never know where it may lead.
- Dress professionally for a networking meeting or event. Unless a casual dress code is stated on the invitation. Remember your business cards, and to say thank you.
- Your network will change. Some of those you meet early on in your career will stay. Whilst others will be replaced by new contacts who will be a better match for the stage you have reached in your journey.

CHAPTER 9

Taking Calculated Risks

In this section, learn how to be comfortable taking risks. This skill can lead to both personal and professional success.

I have taken a lot of risks during my career. Some of them paid off while others didn't, but I don't regret any of them. I wouldn't be where I am today if I hadn't experienced both the positive and negative sides of risk taking. I also find it much easier now to come up with ideas of my own for an adventure!

Be Scared, but Do It Anyway

Making the right decision on whether to take a risk can be difficult. If you don't take it, you could lose an important opportunity for growth, and the competitive advantage this can bring. Whilst it's only natural to be afraid when we are about to enter the unknown. I certainly was, on a number of occasions.

Here are a few examples of what happened to me.

Positive Risks I Have Taken

In September 2019, I auditioned at my local BBC radio station, to join the "New Voices" program. I had done several successful interviews and guest slots on radio, so my confidence had grown. I arrived at the studio two hours before the auditions were due to start. Having imagined some sort of "X-Factor" scenario. With huge crowds and long snake-like queues, I was the first one there. When I realized this meant I would be the first to appear in front of the judges, I began to feel nervous, also secretly a little excited. Even more so when I passed the first stage of the audition, and left the studio on a high. Only to be interviewed then by the BBC, about the experience.

My audition was meant to be a secret, but by the time I got home, I was on the BBC's social media pages and local news. Although I thought it was a success, nothing else happened because of the Covid-19 pandemic. At the time of writing this book, I still haven't been on local radio as a presenter. I couldn't help feeling disappointed and decided to look at what else I could do to satisfy this passion. In 2020, I started The Social Sanctuary podcast. Intending to use this and the experiences I had in school, to support and help other young people like myself to succeed and also to raise awareness of important issues which didn't always get enough airtime.

I focused on having inspirational conversations with key people in the digital world, then went on to cover a variety of topics. Including loneliness awareness week, accepting your sexuality, video games in youth culture, diet shaming, and supporting young people into employment. I met a local podcast expert, James Marriott, through my network and he helped me get my ideas off the ground. James was full of encouragement and positivity. He listened to what I wanted to achieve, and how I was still thinking of working in radio.

I knew that starting the podcast would be a risk. What if no one listened to it? Would I look like a fool? Nevertheless, I carried on, and thankfully, it has proved to be one of the best things I have ever done. I have so far reached more than 4,000 listeners, which is fantastic for a small podcast. It has also helped me find new clients and opportunities on the radio.

Transitioning Into Influencer Marketing

I have always been a huge fan of YouTube. It's how I learned my craft and a lot of the skills I use today in being of service to others. Also, the place I go to when I want to switch off. More often than not I prefer the content produced by YouTubers, to online television and streaming services. I enjoy following my favorite presenters' lives. This sense of connection began when I was at school and university and felt lonely. I regarded the people I followed online as my friends. Even though they didn't know me.

Once I became established as a digital service provider, I recognized a gap in the market. YouTube was booming, and several of my existing clients had asked me how they could collaborate with influencers, to raise awareness of their brands during a marketing campaign. As this was a new area for me, I spent hours studying successful campaigns. Learning how they worked, and charged for paid advertisements, before I started offering this service to my clients. I also focused on researching content creators. Looking to build relationships with those I was following online.

In November 2017, YouTuber Zoella whose real name is Zoe Sugg hits the headlines. Following a public outrage that the £50.00 Advent beauty calendar she was selling only had 12 windows. As this was still trending on Twitter, I decided to write a blog post as quickly as I could, about the hateful abuse she was receiving online. This is an extract from it:

> As someone who works regularly with online influencers and bloggers when creating social media outreach strategies for my clients, it made me think that it's important to respond to this type of bullying. Bloggers and YouTubers can be easy targets because they're the face of their own brands and don't have an institution to hide behind....
>
> My favorite way to look at it is like this: people who dislike you will make you into the person they want you to be, to justify their hatred of you. It's as simple as that....
>
> The bottom line is that our words matter, whether they're typed under the cloak of anonymity or using our real name. How we treat and react to one another is important. As a society, we are more active than ever in the online world and on social media. We have more reach than ever before and have the ability to share our thoughts and opinions with (potentially) millions of people online, from all parts of the world. What kind of digital footprint and impact do you want to have? How can we ensure that we contribute to conversations more respectfully online, even when we are in disagreement? How can we engage ourselves in online activities that foster togetherness and community instead of hate? It's important that you consider all of this before posting something online that could have an impact on someone's entire day, week or life.

Within 10 minutes Zoella's YouTuber boyfriend, Alfie Deyes, retweeted my article. By the end of the day, it had received more than 10,000 views and Zoella had also read it.

I soon received a lot of abuse from Twitter users I didn't know. Accusing me of making their children believe they were bullying one of the celebrities they loved. I also had a lot of messages from journalists, and other celebrities, who had experienced similar negative feedback. They thanked me for writing the article.

I had made a snap decision to share my views on the subject, as an unknown newcomer to the industry, and it paid off. I gained the respect of other professionals who were further on in their careers than I was. All of these helped me establish my profile as a marketing influencer and led to me receiving a lot more enquiries for digital services.

My blog has more than 8,000 views now, which is enough readers to fill Wembley Stadium.

It Was Time to Learn How to Reach Out to Journalists

Not surprisingly, all this left me on an amazing high. I had even been noticed by the two YouTubers I admired the most, and I wanted to stay in the spotlight. So, I started using LinkedIn to talk about other topics, and areas of interest, in which there was something I could say to make an impact. I had seen the positive effect of speaking out against something I didn't believe in and gained the attention of the national press for the first time in my career.

I began chasing more coverage, at every opportunity. This time reaching out to journalists with stories I thought might interest them. Only to receive an endless stream of rejections. This was obviously a hard knock to my confidence, but it taught me that the press wasn't interested in my business if all I wanted was publicity. Journalists would only accept my work if it was in response to stories already in the news or current trends.

I didn't give up, but it took almost 12 months before I got my next piece of press coverage. During this time, I carried on writing about topics I felt passionate about, despite only having a handful of readers. I couldn't help wondering sometimes if this was a complete waste of time and energy. With the benefit of hindsight, I can see that I was finding my voice and giving myself time to grow in the way I needed to for success. Learning to interact with others in the industry I had chosen. While creating a strong platform on which the public would be happy to read, or listen to what I had to say. I had a lot to be thankful for.

My initial strategy back then was to use LinkedIn and e-mail, to reach out to journalists. Simply asking for an opportunity to write for their publications, or if they would be interested in publishing my press releases. Until I discovered that to get the journalist's attention, the e-mail or LinkedIn message had to be personalized, and choosing who to send it to was equally important. So, I started to research the journalist's work before I reached out with my own story. Describing why I believed that he or she was the right person to publish it, and which is a tactic I still use today.

Late in 2018, I received my first reply and an offer of a column in the local newspaper. I couldn't stop jumping for joy! This had happened because I was persistent, had taken the risks I needed to, and responded to current affairs. It was another important step on my career path, and things did get easier after that. At the time of writing this book, I have had more than 70 pieces of amazing press coverage.

Was I Crazy? Not Knowing How to Do It, But Still Saying Yes!

New clients have occasionally asked me about services I didn't offer, and I still quoted a price for the projects. Even though I had no idea how I would go about fulfilling my side of the agreement, which was actually nothing new. I had been learning how to do much of what I achieved since I started my business. However, I still feel very fortunate that this strategy worked most of the time.

Sir Richard Branson said in a tweet, dated January 24th, 2018 that: *"If somebody offers you an amazing opportunity but you are not sure you can do it, say yes – then learn how to do it later!"*

I found it easier to be straight with my clients before I started, so that I could build enough time into the job schedule to get the training I needed. If this should happen to you, don't be alarmed. There are a lot of brilliant, free, and paid, training courses available. After I managed to pull it off, I added these services to those I already offered.

But What About the Negative Risks?

A few that didn't work out as planned are below:

1. **Biting off more than I could chew.** During the Covid-19 lock-down, I lost a lot of regular clients. The future looked grim for UK

businesses that only had a high street presence. In an attempt to help as many as possible get online, I reduced the price of my website design and social media management packages. Launching them as a long-term offer. So that business owners could carry on trading. After only a week, I was inundated with enquiries. It was amazing but, realistically, the offer had generated more work than I could handle.

This turned out to be something that carried on happening, until I learned how to control it. When I had a quiet period, I used to go into panic mode, then launch a special offer with the same result. The problem is I am a massive people pleaser. I don't like saying no, and feeling that I have let anyone down. Until I eventually realized that not being able to give clients my full attention resulted in more disappointment than saying no at the outset would have done. At one point, the sheer number of projects I had to outsource meant I was making barely any profit at all.

2. **My belief in second chances**. Most of the time it is important to give others a second chance. Nevertheless, this practice has caused me a lot of difficulty in the past. For example, the client and I might not have been the best match so we didn't work well together. Or the amount of extra time I had to put in to satisfy his or her unreasonable expectations, and requirements, wasn't in line with what I was being paid.

Yet despite the earlier project having been a nightmare, I still agreed to work with the client again. He or she asked me to because of being satisfied with the service I had provided, but from my point of view, I had to overperform to get this result. Making the job unprofitable. Being faced again with what I regarded as the client's chaotic way of working, I suffered even more stress on the second occasion and found it harder to end the relationship.

3. **App development**. When I was at college and expanding my website design portfolio, I began offering mobile app development as an extra service. After receiving a few enquiries. I believed that this would increase my profit. It was a simple task if the customer already had a website. Nevertheless, the industry was rapidly changing, and I soon felt as if I was facing endless barriers preventing me from delivering the finished product. I also had a number of clients who

were struggling to understand the ever-changing regulations in the app store. As a result, the cost of providing mobile apps and maintaining them continued to rise. I began to operate the service at a loss and had to stop doing it. Even though I had delivered a number of successful apps that I was proud of.

Calculating and Analyzing the Risk

After a while, I learned from the above risks and others I took, that it was important to assess what I was thinking of doing and its chances of success, to avoid paying the price later.

So, before I make a start now, I plan as far as possible what will be involved, also consider the potential cost, and benefit of taking the risk if I achieve what I want to. In an attempt to reduce uncertainty, and set up a strategy for success.

The following are key questions to consider before you go ahead:

- What are the strengths and weaknesses in taking the risk, including financial and legal implications?
- How will the outcome of the risk help you to achieve your goals, long-term career, or business plans?
- What are the measured steps you will need to take along the way, to achieve the outcome you are looking for?
- What will be the effect of taking the risk on your business, and you personally, at each stage in the process?
- Does the risk align with your values, and mission statement?

Takeaways

- Be careful not to over promise, then underdeliver. Not only do you run the risk of having to give refunds, but also this can harm your professional reputation.
- When the going gets tough, don't give up! Carry on taking risks, and you will eventually hit the jackpot. I also don't have to chase journalists now to get coverage. ...They come to me.

CHAPTER 10

Working in Small Chunks

Breaking Down Tasks Into Manageable Parts

You'll find running a business is easier when you have smaller, more manageable, parts to work with and can put similar activities into groups. This is how I organized what I wanted to say into a book. The chunks became pages, then chapters. I knew that writing it would be a long project so I needed a plan, and to make sure I didn't forget to include any of the content I wanted to. Doing it this way also makes it easier to work on more than one project at a time.

You can use this process in any area of your life, personally or professionally. Consider first of all how much time you can devote to each project or parts of it, and apportion your day or week accordingly. Don't forget to factor in rest and relaxation, also exercise.

A Great Routine Is an Asset

My parents brought me up to always have a good routine. Irrespective of the stage I had reached in my life. They told me to make the most of every second I had and go outside every day to get some fresh air. Even though I knew this was great advice, I sometimes felt that it didn't do me any favors. I am always busy and use the little spare time I have to plan. So, you'll rarely find me at home doing nothing. Nevertheless, they were absolutely right! Having a good routine is vitally important, especially when you are self-employed.

People's idea of a freelancer can be someone who only works when they have to. Taking long breaks for hours on end to see friends and have fun. Whilst this couldn't be further from the truth for most of the freelancers I know. Being self-employed does bring a certain amount of freedom, but if we take a few hours off during the day, it usually means working longer at night and on weekends.

Takeaways

- When you are creating chunks of time, write down everything you do in a day or week. Then look at the activities you can omit, cut down, or would like to include. This will help you create a good personal, and professional routine.
- Don't forget to include a chunk of time for life administration. Such as paying bills, going to the supermarket, and so on.
- After a while, your routine will be just what you do, but don't be afraid to make changes to its structure. However, if you break your routine by not sticking to it this also creates change, and it may be difficult to get back on track again. Especially if you leave it for a long time.
- Sticking to a good routine can have huge benefits for mental health, helping to reduce stress and anxiety. Creating certainty in what can be an unpredictable world.
- A routine can boost productivity by helping you focus on the things that matter the most to you, including goals. Even let you find space for what you didn't think you had enough time to do.

PART 4

Next Steps

CHAPTER 11

Turning Competitors, and Customers, Into Cheerleaders

In this section, learn the importance of the three "Cs." How to take a positive view of competitors and accept the support which customers and they can give to your business. Making them your greatest cheerleaders!

The Importance of Building Good Business Relationships

It took me a long time to realize that I was only competing with myself. No one else. Even though initially I couldn't stop comparing myself to others. Despite the majority being much older, and that they had been in business for a long time. ...This was the wrong approach to take.

When I was 18 years old, I found myself in a toxic friendship with someone I met while networking. This person appeared to be highly respected by my contacts. Nevertheless, he often made me feel as if I hadn't earned my success and wasn't quite good enough. I tried hard to keep up with his champagne lifestyle, the nice car, and the collection of designer suits. Buying things that I couldn't afford, so that by the time I was 19, I had ended up in a mountain of debt.

I found a second job during the summer break from university, to start paying everything off. I also had to swallow my pride. I worked in a factory that was far removed from everything I enjoyed doing, but I am so grateful now to have learned this lesson at an early age. Also, I had the support of others, who genuinely wanted to help me turn things around. This experience taught me two very important lessons:

- Debt soon builds, and you should never purchase anything just to keep up with someone else or their opinion of you. If you can't meet the repayments, it can soon become unmanageable, then snowball. Impacting all areas of your life.
- Comparing yourself to others only makes you feel miserable. It's far better instead to think of others' success as motivation to work harder and do better. So that you can afford to buy what they have.

Once I had cleared the debt, I found it difficult to trust any of the other competitors I met. Until I discovered the Being Freelance Community on Facebook. I began to change my mind once I realized there was plenty of work for everyone, and I could look to them for guidance. Giving the "been there, done that" sort of advice, and more importantly, help me with referrals. As soon as I took this more positive approach, I made some amazing friends and contacts in the community. I even featured on the Being Freelance Podcast with founder, Steve Folland, who gives so much of his time and energy to supporting other freelancers and those starting out in business.

By opening up in this way I allowed my business to grow, and I am often the one now who is fully booked, with the ability to refer work to others.

Good business relationships are based on honesty and trust. Not only with others but also with yourself too. It's important to be honest about the parts of the business you enjoy, and those you would rather delegate, then action this. Conversely, if your business collaborator is doing something you don't agree with, speak up! Honesty is always the best policy. It is important too, to be clear on setting expectations. When you both know where you stand, you'll feel much more invested, and aligned, to getting the result you want.

Building a community of supporters is crucial if you want to grow and flourish. Referrals help cement these relationships and work both ways. So, if you see an opportunity that you can't take on, but one of your competitors can, refer and tell them about it.

Gathering Testimonials

This is essentially an endorsement or recommendation, based on your client or customer's positive experience of your product or service. It can be done in text, as a photograph, audio recording, or video and you can obtain them in different ways. For example, turning satisfied customers into case studies for your website or marketing. Also using specific messages as a testimonial, comments on your blog, or reviews left about your services on external sites like Yelp. Seeking your client or customer's permission, to use any of these in this way.

My process for gathering testimonials has changed over the years. I used to reach out to clients via e-mail and ask for a testimonial which I would upload to my website. When review platforms started to appear I chose a free one which again worked for me, and I began to accept reviews from there. Fast forward to today, and I have built up a collection of testimonials across various platforms.

I would recommend collecting Google reviews as your first choice and ensuring you have a Google business profile. You don't need a physical address to set one up, and it's free. Lots of people will do a Google search for your business, before deciding whether to work with you. It's equally important that you have a positive selection of reviews next to your business name on Google.

After a while, I hired a professional to create testimonial videos for me. The earlier videos consisted of shots of me, with client testimonials below, as I worked in my hometown. This was a very powerful sales tool and an easy way to showcase my reputation to prospective clients. Making the investment in time, and cost, well worth it.

Takeaways

- Building a career or business takes time, and entrepreneurship isn't a race.
- Use a sample letter or request template when you ask for a testimonial. Alternatively, use a plugin or software to help you collect testimonials from different platforms.

CHAPTER 12

Dealing With Copycats

I have had my fair share of people copying what I do in business over the years. It has usually been someone I worked with or met at an event. When you see a competitor set up a similar business and offer the same services as you do, it can be beyond frustrating.

However, another way of looking at it is that this sort of competition can also be healthy. It stops us from becoming complacent and can lead to having a stronger, more resilient, business in the long term. It may even help to raise awareness of and grow your niche, creating more opportunities for everyone.

I have found the best way forward is to acknowledge the copycat's presence, then try to ignore it. As you become even better at understanding your own customers' needs and delivering more of the same. Leaving any copycat competitors far behind. Whilst turning what was an annoying situation into something much more positive.

A lot of entrepreneurs understandably find it difficult to do this, and I did at first. Especially when you have invested so much time, energy, and hard work into creating a unique brand. With great slogans, a logo, and distinct voice. You may have built a strong following and were secretly pleased at how successful the business had become. Only to start seeing someone else using your work online, but don't worry.

There are steps you can take to protect your brand, and make sure you stay on top:

- **Make Your Brand Unique**
  Focus your energy on standing out from the crowd. If you are just starting out, you may need to create a unique name for your business. It can be tempting to use a generic one, but there is likely to be a lot of other people doing the same. Also, try to create something different for your logo, so avoid clip

art and stock images. Again, these are often overused. If you can afford to, hire a professional graphic designer to do the work for you. Treat your slogans, and messages in the same way. Making sure you are saying something different, and unique.

- **Keep It in Perspective**

  If the copycat persists, you can post publicly on social media, and talk about what is happening. To make it more difficult for him or her to keep up the charade, before you resort to legal action if this is something you have decided to do.

  Nevertheless, it is important to keep things in perspective. Copycats can be frustrating, but they are not the end of the world. If your own business is still growing or doing well, and sales haven't deteriorated. Remember too, that it's a sign of success when people try to imitate you. It means that you have created something valuable, that others are taking notice of, which is the ultimate business goal.

- **Protecting Your Reputation**

  If you haven't already done so, register a trademark for your brand so that you can take legal action more easily. Then contact the other business owner, and let him or her know you are unhappy that your brand and copy are being used without your permission. The business owner might be willing to stop.

  Also make sure that you are using the same name, and logo, across all of your own social media accounts. To ensure that anyone who searches for your brand will find the same information on these sites. It's a good idea to stay active on social media if you have a copycat, to prevent him or her from stealing this spotlight from you.

- Show new clients or customers that you are the real deal Don't give up! Showcase your experience and expertise, by creating brilliant content that highlights your knowledge and skills. Remember to include a link to your website and social media accounts, so that people can find you more easily.

Also make time to build relationships with influencers, and potential new customers or clients. Offer to collaborate, and reach out on social media. It will help to spread the word that this is your brand.

Takeaways

- It's easy to jump to conclusions, so check carefully before taking action, that this really is a copycat situation. Look at the other website and all of the social media accounts. If the competitor is using a similar name, logo, and slogans as you then it is likely that your brand is being copied.
- You may find it useful to talk to a mentor or one of your supporters, if you are struggling to deal with this situation. To help you decide what action to take, if any.

CHAPTER 13

Investing to Grow

When it's a question of whether to spend money to make money, as people often say you should, this can be a bit of a conundrum. You want to be successful but may not have the resources or capital to invest.

In my experience, if you want your business to grow and flourish, it is a good idea to invest in it. If you can't afford to do this, there are a lot of free tools and resources available online. Making the investment time, not money related. Unless of course you lose profit, or money you would have earned, at the same time as you use one of them. Here are the best ways you can invest in the future of your personal business:

- The most important investment is always in yourself. When you take the time to learn new skills and develop your expertise. Also network to make connections, while marketing the business and your brand.
- The right online tools and resources can help you save valuable time and make more money in the long run. A good website is one of the best investments you can make. One that is well designed, to showcase your work and services, can help you attract more clients. Remember that investing in a good logo and branding will also help you stand out from the competition.
- A strong marketing strategy can help you reach more people and grow your business. Also help you start to build better relationships with potential clients, and customers.
- Getting the right technology and software for your business can help you become more efficient and productive. For example, by automating some of your processes to save time, and the frustration of having to repeat mundane tasks when you already have a busy schedule.

It's important to assess the risks of investing, preferably before you commit to doing it. Then the return on the amount you have invested. So that you can keep an eye on how much money you are spending and making as a result. Helping you determine whether or not the investment was worthwhile. You can do this by tracking your online ROI results, and seeing if they are helping you reach your goal.

The Importance of Upskilling

When it comes to self-employment, the advantages are clear. You have the ability to choose when and where you work, also the rates you charge. You will more than likely have to contend with a large number of competitors. So, it's vital for any business owner or freelancer to stay on the cutting edge of his or her game to optimize retention and opportunities for growth.

Upskilling empowers us to stay effective and focused. As we develop and hone existing talents, or learn new skills. Possibly to cover a gap in the market.

Are you starting out in the web development field, and looking for a website development proposal template? It could be that you are a UI/UX designer wishing to transfer to front-end development (or the other way around). There is currently a heightened demand for certain competencies, like JavaScript and CSS programming, social media marketing, and creating Shopify stores.

When you have finished your course and received a certification, you can include this in your resume or portfolio. Making you a more desirable candidate when applying for a job or investment.

How to Stay Up to Date With Business Trends

- Keep an eye on social media influencers, those who are further up the career ladder than yourself, or have achieved what you aspire to.
- Subscribe to relevant newsletters, so that you get regular updates.
- Read blog articles that have received positive feedback.
- Sign up for a publication, in print or digital.

- Tune into podcasts, when the host and guests talk about topical issues related to the industry you are in.
- Acquire knowledge from talking to your peers as you network, on LinkedIn, or online. Why not sign up for the next event in your area of expertise, and stay behind afterward? To talk to the other attendees and speakers. You may well learn a lot from doing this.
- If you are someone who enjoys (or needs) to stay at home, Zoom and Microsoft Teams are other great tools to use. You can join in webinars from your living room. Make sure to switch your computer microphone back on when the Q&A session begins, and don't be afraid to ask questions, if you have any. It's another fantastic way to learn what you want, or need to know.

Ways of Assessing the Return on Your Investments

This will depend on your goals or vision for the future, and the reason why you made the investment. If it was solely to increase revenue and profit as quickly as possible, this may be reflected almost immediately in the entries in your business accounts or bank statements. For example, monies received from new or existing clients for an extra service you now offer because of upskilling.

This might also give you an indication of whether you will be likely to meet the projection you made in your business plan. In relation to where you would like to see your business growth in five to 10 years' time. Should the level of new clients you have attracted continue, because of this extra service you are now offering.

Other Advantages of Investing Available Funds, or Time to Upskill Include

- Diversifying, and expanding your portfolio, which is essential for building a successful freelance career.
- Demonstrating your expertise in different areas can help to increase your credibility in the marketplace, and make you stand out from the competition.

- Achieving success in life largely depends on feeling content with what we do. By gaining new capabilities you can experience an increase in self-esteem, assurance, and general mental health. This may be reflected in improved performance, enthusiasm, and commitment to your freelance job or business.
- Freelancers and business owners decide how much they will charge for their services. However, background and proficiency need to be taken into account when doing this. Investing in yourself, and improving your skills, can enable you to raise your fees. As you will be providing a much more valuable service.

How I Invested in My Business, and Myself

My biggest personal investments have been in my website, marketing, and public relations to raise my profile. I have also invested in a business coach since I suffered a burnout in late, 2019. Working with Helen Campbell has been one of the most powerful investments I ever made. She has helped me to transform my work–life balance, and it's been great to have a coach as a cheerleader. Supporting me in winning new clients, bettering myself, and challenging me about the decisions I make. Mostly, however, ensuring that I always put myself first, which is very important and can easily be forgotten when you are growing a business.

Needless to say, not all of the investments I made have been worthwhile. There were the courses I signed up for, and didn't have time to complete, and membership organizations I joined without using any of the benefits.

However, looking back now at my career, and business journey, I can't stress enough that the best investment I made was always in myself. It will probably be the same for you. Whether your aim is to improve your mental health or raise your business profile, it will help you reap the rewards of your hard work and ongoing success.

Takeaway

- Don't just plan to invest time and funds into your career or business, make sure you also put what you have decided to do in your diary. So that you attend networking events, do the modules on a course that will be beneficial, read the industry journals you have subscribed to, and so on. Also, give yourself time afterward to consider how what you have learned is beneficial, and again, an opportunity to put this knowledge into practice. Whether you can do this immediately, or if it needs to be done in stages.

CHAPTER 14

How to Get Funding for Your Business

I have never had a business loan or worked with an investor. Except when I entered the BiG Challenge competition at school and received a £25.00 loan. I repaid £30.00, including interest.

I have instead received a number of grants, which I didn't have to pay back. I was also fortunate to be eligible for government support during the pandemic. Followed by two local authority grants, as part of its business support program. The first was for a new website, and the second was to increase my profile locally.

This funding has been an enormous help to me in getting started as an entrepreneur, for which I am very grateful.

What Is a Grant?

Essentially, it's funding given to entrepreneurs or small business owners by the government, a company, philanthropist, or publicly funded scheme which doesn't need to be repaid. The amount can vary from hundreds to thousands of pounds.

You also don't need to repay any interest, give away equity in your business, or go through as many checks to access the funding. Making a grant a fantastic option for start-ups. You can invest the money you receive in upskilling, materials, employees, training, or equipment.

The awards are usually made to encourage promising talent, provide an opportunity to pursue entrepreneurship, help new innovative programs become more widely known, fund worthy environmental or other purpose-driven projects, and stimulate the economy. Each grant will have a different application process, entry criteria, and requirements to fulfill. However, getting the award is clearly worth the effort.

Applying for a Grant

Do some research, first of all, to find the best available grant for your business, before you start sending out applications. There is no point in applying to a scheme if you aren't eligible, or it doesn't match your needs. For example, The Prince's Trust has a specific age bracket for applicants.

To Give Your Application the Best Shot, Make Sure You Have

- A thorough, and up to date, business plan.
- A detailed breakdown of how you intend to use the funds.
- A good account of your business history, to help persuade the awarding body that you will behave responsibly with the funding. (Good accounting software can make this task a lot easier.)
- An outline view of how the organization will meet its objectives in giving you the funding.

After This, My Top Tips for Making the Application Are

1. To apply, as soon as possible: Especially when the application process first opens. Make sure you keep an eye on the space, so you know when a relevant grant is coming up.
2. Try to make a personal contact at the awarding body before you apply: Then if there are any problems, or your application doesn't seem to be progressing, you will have someone to call who knows you. He or she may be able to give you some personalized advice.
3. Consider appointing a grant consultant or working with a business support advisor: He or she can help you find the grants best suited to you, saving you hours of research. Also have a better chance of communicating with the organization and keeping tabs on the progress of your application. However, there are some awarding bodies that don't accept applications submitted through consultancies, so take this advice on a case-by-case basis. Your local council or government will usually offer business support advice, and they can often advise you on any available funding.

4. Pay close attention to the grant's objectives: For example, if an awarding body wants to fund innovative solutions to the technological skills gap in the United Kingdom, highlight and emphasize how your business is doing this. Be clear on the benefits your business will bring to the area covered by the grant and explain that you need the money to fulfill these specific objectives.

5. Don't be untruthful: If you need to bend the facts about your business, so that it will match the grant's criteria, it's probably not the right one for you.

Every grant process is different so there isn't a set time when you can expect to receive a decision. Applications made to your local authority or an enterprise partnership, for example, could be resolved in a matter of weeks or even days. Whilst national organizations and European bodies can take months to reply.

What Will the Awards Committee Be Looking for?

The eligibility criteria for a grant usually include questions about:

- The purpose of your business: The industry you are operating in or plan to, the problem you are tackling, and the impact you want your business to have.
- Where you are located: Separate regions across the United Kingdom have their own awarding bodies or schemes which focus solely on companies in that specific area.
- The size of your business: Certain schemes are restricted to businesses that have less than 250 employees. While others only deal with those which have fewer than say 50, 20, or 10 employees.
- How long you have been trading.

I recommend looking at grant funding first, before you think of taking out a loan. However, if your business does need a considerable amount of investment, to grow or start-up, a loan or finding an investor may well be the best option.

Applying for a Business Loan

Here are my top tips to consider, if you are applying for a small business loan:

- Research the types of loans which are available.
- Explore government and private loan options.
- Don't be afraid to shop around.
- Make sure you have good credit.
- Consider the loan amount you need.
- Have a plan for using the loan funds.
- Develop a comprehensive business plan.
- Have a detailed understanding of your cash flow.
- Have a clear understanding of the terms of the loan.
- Understand the repayment schedule.
- Be prepared to provide collateral.
- Be wary of additional fees, and closing costs.

You will need to demonstrate that you can repay the loan and regular installments. This is the primary concern of lenders. As a new business owner, it can be difficult to establish your ability to do this. So, make sure that you provide comprehensive financial information in your business plan. Don't overestimate your goals, but be realistic. If you have been in business for a while and can show that your income exceeds your outgoings, have available evidence to support this.

Entrepreneurs often don't have sufficient assets in their businesses to guarantee a loan. When this happens any joint applicants (including you), associates, friends, or family members who agree to secure the loan will need to use personal property as collateral, which is likely to be lost if the loan isn't repaid.

Be open and honest about your financial circumstances. Not everyone can boast a pristine credit history and financial background. If you have an issue that could potentially affect your application, it's best to be candid about it right away. This doesn't always mean you won't qualify, and being truthful shows that you are reliable. It's much better to provide information upfront than have to explain this during the process.

Be sensible when it comes to how much you should borrow. Make sure you ask for an adequate amount of funds, either through debt or equity, to set up and sustain your business at the beginning but don't take on so much that you can't meet the repayments.

Don't expect the lender to provide the entire funding for your business. You may need to invest your own capital and have access to other sources of financing. So that you can cover any unexpected expenses while still paying off the loan.

You also need to know what to include in a business plan. Essentially, it should cover your objectives, strategies, sales, marketing, and financial forecasts. Whilst there are several different structures you could use for the plan; the primary focus is on demonstrating how well you know your own business and the industry. Also making sure that your predictions for financial success are substantiated by the accounts you provide or thorough research. Don't be alarmed by this!

You don't need to be an expert in financial matters, but knowing how to read and explain financial accounts and reports will be helpful.

You should also understand the different types of business loans you can apply for. Banks can offer low-interest loans and lines of credit, as they lend to organizations with a good credit rating, and these are sanctioned by the government. Regrettably, however, not all small businesses meet these standards. Banks also provide credit cards. Although the interest rates can be higher, and reach 18 to 29 percent if payments are not made on time.

It's important to be wary when taking out a loan. Make certain that you understand the real interest rate you will be paying. There are numerous choices available for small business loans, particularly from the Internet or nonbank lenders. These associations are not supervised, and some employ diverse systems to work out a "factor rate." While these rates may appear very low at first glance, when you compute the corresponding annual percentage rate (APR), you get a very different result. Often in the high double digits, or even three digits!

Working With Investors

- An investor may be more prepared to take a risk, for example, on poor credit ratings if he or she feels your business has great potential.
- You won't necessarily have tight deadlines for the repayment of capital and interest.
- You will gain access to the investor's knowledge, expertise, and contacts. Any of which can be a valuable asset.
- The investor's own success can help to motivate you.
- His or her involvement in your business can make other stakeholders, clients, and customers feel confident about working with you.

Start-up business owners will more likely find success with a business angel. As they typically back businesses at an early stage. Instead of a traditional investor who is often employed by a venture capital or private equity firm, is responsible for investing other people's money, and works within a more rigid structure. Business angels on the other hand come from a variety of backgrounds. They can operate individually, or as part of a syndicate, investing their own money.

The UK Business Angels Association effectively operates as the UK's trade association, with 650 members who invested £2.3bn last year. If you are outside the United Kingdom, the Angel Investment Network and Angel Capital Association, both of which are based in the United States, have many members who invest on a global basis.

A crucial question to ask the business angel is how hands on will he or she wants to be. In some cases, angels are looking to operate as more or less silent partners. Leaving the entrepreneur to run the business on a day-to-day basis. Others are looking for much more involvement. Even though they don't want to take on an operational role, they still expect to be consulted regularly and be involved with key strategic decisions.

You need to be clear about the sort of business relationship you want in working with an investor. If you are looking for active and regular support, a silent partner isn't likely to provide this. On the other hand, if funding is the main priority, having a more involved business angel may cause tension between you. Given these nuances, it is important that entrepreneurs, and potential angel investors, take a little time to build a relationship before sealing the deal. Anywhere between three and six months is typical.

The conversation doesn't have to be exclusive. There is nothing to stop business owners exploring investment opportunities with several angels, before making a final decision.

Takeaways

- Do the research before you apply for funding. Ultimately, choose the most suitable source of funding for your business, and financial status.
- You might like to consider involving a coapplicant if your credit score isn't satisfactory, or you lack collateral.
- You might find it helpful to take advice from others with more experience than yourself, a mentor, or a professional accountant. To ensure that the amount you are intending to borrow is reasonable, and that it will meet your needs, with affordable repayments.

CHAPTER 15

Side Hustles

Other Ways of Making Money

I'm a huge fan of the side hustle! I don't believe in placing limitations on what we can or can't do, so I have tried a lot of them in business. Not all of them were a success, but it was a great way to do something different, without the pressure of it being a main source of income. The Social Sanctuary podcast I started during the Covid-19 lockdown is an example of one of my side hustles, which I am still very glad I did.

I have also tried running online e-learning courses, alongside my regular digital services. I spent a long time designing a social media masterclass, a few years ago. The first webinar I ran was a huge success, with 15 attendees. As it had the potential to generate a good income, I decided to run them on a monthly basis. Unfortunately, it proved to be a one-hit wonder, as no one else signed up to attend. Despite the good feedback, I had received initially, and trying everything I could to sell tickets. Nevertheless, there is always something you can take from a negative situation. The material I developed for the masterclass is still useful today, as a marketing resource for clients who are developing their strategies.

Affiliate marketing and schemes are another brilliant way to generate extra income. I signed up in the early days of the Amazon Associate program and earned between 5 and 10 percent commission on the products which my IT support customers purchased. After I had an appointment with them or made a recommendation. I still occasionally earn a small amount from affiliate marketing. Even though I don't actively promote it. I also used to receive a £50.00 Amazon gift card every quarter. The beauty of affiliate marketing schemes is that they are often free to do, and take minimal effort to be profitable. All you need to do is generate affiliate links and send these to your customers.

I have had a number of part-time roles alongside my business when there was a quiet spell, and in the early days, if I wasn't generating enough money to make self-employment my full-time role. I have done everything from working as a technical support advisor for a large electrical retailer to working in a swimming pool and leisure center as a receptionist. Also helped out in a supermarket cash office, and as a health and safety officer.

More recently, I took a role as a search engine optimization and marketing executive in a local escape room, because of my huge passion for the leisure and tourism industry. The job came along after I had just graduated from university and was finding working at home every day a little lonely. I only worked there for two days a week. I also knew that I could use the experience to broaden my skills and build new connections.

My role was made redundant during the pandemic. Nevertheless, I learned a lot from my time there, and I made some amazing friends. The workplace was occasionally toxic, but I regarded this again as part of my learning experience. It helped me gain a better understanding of my personal values, and what I really wanted to do.

As we were about to enter a second lockdown in the United Kingdom, at the end of 2020, an unexpected opportunity came along. I was invited to support one of my social media clients for two days a week, in developing a marketing strategy. At the time I didn't really have the capacity to take on the project, but I really enjoyed working with this particular client, and it felt like the right thing to do. Especially given the uncertainty all of us were facing at the time.

I had also learned from my experience at the escape room that I preferred to be self-employed, if possible, and I wanted to keep this particular client on a retainer basis. As a result, I promised myself that I would honor the commitment for a year, which ended in me working with the client for just over two years, and it felt great to have this change of focus.

I have learned that being a sole trader can be a quiet, and lonely place. It can also have variety and be beneficial for personal growth. Especially when we decide to have a side hustle that allows us to expand and build our networks. Or at least have a change of scenery, which helps to keep ideas for the future fresh, and unique.

My current side hustle is to expand my own social media presence. It's difficult doing this, at the same time as managing my clients' social media pages. I particularly want to expand into TikTok and find the time to continue developing my YouTube presence.

Here Are a Few More Ideas of Things to Do, If You Want a Side Hustle

- Dog walking can be a brilliant service to offer, if you enjoy being around animals and keeping fit.
- Cleaning, or doing odd jobs. Like building flat-pack furniture, hanging pictures, clearing out a garage, and so on. Be creative with the services you offer. You may be surprised by what you can come up with.
- Delivery work, if you have a valid UK driving license for a car or motorcycle. Ranging from takeaways to delivering parcels as a courier. Don't forget to factor in petrol, and insurance costs if you are using your own vehicle.
- You'll find opportunities for bar work, waiting tables, or other hospitality roles on social media and the main job sites. Like Indeed, and Total Jobs.
- Selling your unwanted belongings on eBay or local sites. Going to auctions, and sourcing charity shops for bargains you can resell at a profit.
- Registering with a staffing agency to do temporary or short-term contract jobs. For example, office work or typing.

Takeaway

- Be brave! Life is an adventure, and truly what we make it. You never know what you will learn, or who you are going to meet when you have a side hustle. ...The extra money is fantastic too.

CHAPTER 16

Entering Competitions to Win an Award

As you know my first experience of winning an award was at school in 2012, with the BiG Challenge competition. I learned then that even if you don't win, simply entering can be a huge boost to your self-esteem. It's the most important part, also making sure to stay humble when celebrating success, not boast about it.

I sold keyrings and greetings cards back then, with my friend, Gabe. Just before the spring break we were shortlisted for an award and asked to prepare a presentation to the panel of judges and business experts. I was both terrified and excited. Naturally, I was reliant on Gabe for support. Also, my teacher, Jackie Goodrum, and Jo Silverwood who was the School Enterprise Co-Ordinator. They helped to build my confidence and made sure I practiced until I knew my pitch by heart. I can still remember standing in the classroom alongside Gabe. With them watching us. My legs were trembling, and I couldn't get my words out. Doubting my ability to do it.

However, after lots of practice and injecting a little humor into the situation, I started to feel as if we might have a chance after all. Gabe and I spent all of our spring break preparing, and anticipating what giving the presentation would be like. Then before we knew it, we were on our way to the Town Hall, to join other schools and colleges from across the city.

Halfway through my introduction, I realized that I had never been as nervous before, but when Gabe began to speak, I started to feel calmer. It seemed like a breeze after that, and even our jokes went down well. All of our hard work had paid off, because a couple of weeks later our invitation to the awards ceremony arrived, and we were ecstatic.

It was great because our families were also invited. It was the first time we had to wear a suit, and it was a very special occasion. Although we knew that we had won, the prize was still a mystery. Nevertheless, I felt really proud. Not only because of what Gabe and I had achieved but also that I had gone outside of my comfort zone to do it.

We had a brilliant evening and won the Best Presentation to The Judges award, and Third Prize for our age category. I was most proud of the Best Presentation award. We were selected from over 30 shortlisted teams, and this meant a lot. I felt that I had proved to all of my peers who had bullied me, and thought I wasn't going to make anything of myself because I was too nervous, that they had been wrong. We could go back to school and show everyone our trophies, along with the gift cards we had won. Including the teachers who hadn't been like Jackie and Jo, but dismissed me. Getting these awards boosted my confidence. I was hoping now to gain everyone's respect, and it felt amazing!

The grand prize for the competition was always a holiday to Dubai. So, I re-entered every year until 2015. Continuing to win prizes with my IT support venture, but not the holiday. This sometimes made me feel that I had failed. I was the only student to enter on so many consecutive occasions. However, looking back, I had actually achieved much more than this. After I entered the competition for the last time, I realized that the holiday didn't matter. How far I had come was worth so much more to those around me, and myself.

I learned later that there was a lot of internal politics which affected the final decision on the winning team, and that it wasn't always about the entrants. So, I returned to the competition in 2016, as a sponsor. It's now run by our local authority, and I am on the steering committee. This is my way of giving back to students. Ensuring they get the same experiences I had, without any political or social bias, related to their school or economic status.

I won another award in 2013 for the first mobile app I developed. It was for a new market in Sheffield City Centre. It took me several weeks to work on it, and I won first place. When the Business Manager at my school saw what I had created, he commissioned me to develop another one. Aimed at enabling my school to send messages to parents, and for the local community to find out what was happening during term time. I was paid just over £700.00 for this project, which was a lot of money for a 15 years old to earn, and I was thrilled. Also, the app was being used to help others in my community, which wouldn't have happened if I hadn't entered the competitions.

I used the school app then to enter a regional coding competition later in the year, and I won another two prizes, including £300.00. Also, some work experience with a professional app development company, to further my skills and learning.

While I was a student at Sheffield Hallam University, I was lucky enough to win some of my biggest awards to date. Sadly, during my first term at university, I was still on a low ebb due to the effects of the toxic relationship I mentioned earlier with the person I met while networking. As you know I had a huge amount of debt to pay off, while trying to reset my life. Nevertheless, I persevered, and during my second semester, I discovered that the University had an enterprise team of amazing advisers. Supporting student, and graduate entrepreneurs to grow their businesses. It was through this that I met Rob King, one of the advisers, who would play an important part in my business growth and future success.

This proved to be another example of how the right person can come into your life at the right time. I started to meet Rob on a one-to-one basis once a month, and he told me about an upcoming competition for student and graduate entrepreneurs. It involved pitching their businesses to a live audience, for the chance to win up to £5,000.00 in funding. Following his advice, I entered the Hallam Enterprise Awards later that year and was lucky enough to win £1,000.00 prize money. After being voted the Best Pitch Award. Again, although I was hugely thankful for it, I gained so much more than the prize money when I entered this competition. I made some fantastic friends. Also built valuable relationships with graphic designers and people in business whom I would later come to work with.

Rob forwarded an e-mail to me, the following year. Inviting applicants to enter a national competition, the IPSE (Association of Independent Professionals and the Self-Employed) Awards, which represents UK freelancers and those who are self-employed. The deadline for entries was on the same day that Rob had sent the e-mail to me, but something told me that I needed to park all of my plans for the afternoon and apply. I had never entered a national competition before, but after my success in the Hallam Enterprise Awards, I felt that I had just as much of a chance as anyone else.

I spent the rest of the day in the university library, completing my application, and I hit send at the last minute. I had forgotten about it when an e-mail landed in my inbox, a couple of months later. Inviting me to London to pitch to a panel of business experts and high-profile freelancers. This was really exciting! The presentation was on the final day of my first year at university. I had an examination in the morning before I headed down to London to give my pitch. Looking back now, I am not sure how I managed to do both on the same day, and the judges were impressed that I had turned up. I practiced my pitch for two hours on the train, and the five minutes I had to impress the judges flew by once I was in front of them. I met lots of lovely freelancers that day, who had also been shortlisted. There was such a positive energy in the waiting room, while we supported each other.

A week later, I learned that I was one of the final four candidates for the Young Freelancer of the Year award. I was invited to London again and stayed at a hotel for the night to celebrate my achievements. My parents couldn't make it so I invited Rob, my Business Adviser, to celebrate with me. It was a summer evening, and we enjoyed a glass or two of champagne by the River Thames. I remember feeling calm, and irrespective of the result, honored to be a part of it. I had replayed my name being announced as the winner, over and over again in my thoughts. Until it reached the point where it felt like it had already happened.

I took my seat and watched the other freelancers collect their awards. Then, to my utter amazement, my name was called as the winner of the Young Freelancer of the Year award. I felt overwhelmed and thrilled, when I collected my £3,000.00 prize. I also received a coaching session with a business growth adviser, and one year of IPSE membership.

It was the first time I had received national recognition for the work I was doing part-time, alongside my studies as a student. It made me ask the question: Shouldn't this be my ultimate goal? It's a huge confidence boost, hearing others you don't know telling you that you can make it. Strangers, the judges, and people really high up in the industry. It completely changed my mindset. I had received a stamp of approval on a national level, for all of the work I had put in up to that point.

I remember leaving the celebration, and bursting into tears as I told my parents over the phone that I had won. I found it very difficult to compose myself afterward. It felt as if I had proved that I could still make something of myself. Even after all of the setbacks I had experienced earlier in my life. That night, I slept with my IPSE trophy, and it took me a long time to believe it was real.

There are so many awards for businesses and freelancers. Where you can nominate yourself, or others can do it for you. I have been lucky enough to experience the latter on two occasions. In 2019 when I won the Ambassador of the Year award for Youth Employment UK, I mentioned earlier. This was a huge surprise, and an honor, also a fantastic reward for all of the voluntary hours I had put in. Not that I ever expected anything in return.

Then just before I finished my course at Sheffield Hallam University, I was nominated by the university staff and students to receive an Inspirational Student Award for Enterprise and Entrepreneurship because of my achievements. If only I had known this was going to happen when I was very nervous during my first year, and wondering sometimes if I could carry on.

As you can see from my story, the benefits of entering for an award can go far beyond having a trophy to display. Whether we win, are shortlisted, or simply manage to get a submission completed these are all important steps in our personal and business growth.

Why You Should Nominate Yourself for an Award

I am wondering now as I write this, whether you have considered entering for any awards. If not, I guess you may have found yourself making excuses like:

- My schedule is too full!
- There's no point! I'll never win.
- My lack of expertise limits me.
- What good would it do?

There is a long list of reasons why you shouldn't bother doing it, but even better ones for why you should.

After winning my awards, I noticed an improvement in the quality of my work because I did feel more confident. I knew that I was doing my best, but when someone else publicly acknowledged that I was doing well, this proved to be a real motivator. The application process makes you think about, and celebrate again, all of the good things that you have achieved. At the very least it's worth entering, to prove to yourself just how far you have come.

I know that you have done loads of great stuff, but filling out an application for an award will encourage you to acknowledge this. Also, some of the things you did, which you possibly thought were only okay, were actually brilliant! And guess what? *Spoiler alert....*

They were more than likely brilliant, to begin with.

This is my take on it:

- The truth of the matter is YOU MIGHT WIN! (But you definitely won't, if you don't enter.)
- Even if you don't win, entering can lead to a lot of good things happening:
  (a) Instead of just doing the work, applying makes you think about your business, and define your goals.
  (b) Business growth.
  (c) Unexpected opportunities coming your way.
  (d) Gaining credibility in the eyes of your competitors, customers, and clients.
  (e) It's great to meet new people, expand your contact list, and network.

Whether it's freelancer awards, small business or chamber of commerce awards, location-specific awards in your city or county, magazine/blog awards, or your own industry-specific accolades.... Take action now, and enter. The likelihood of you succeeding is higher than you might imagine.

Making an Impact on the Judges

Here are a few top tips for when you go in front of the panel, to show them that your entry is exceptional:

1. Demonstrate the truth of what you said in your application. That you provide a stellar service, offer the best value for money, and so

on. You can prove these claims, with reports and data. Such as competitor analysis and sales, turnover, and profit cost figures.

2. There are numerous ideas that may seem great but have not been successful in practice. So, it's important to show that your product or service has an audience, and that your venture is profitable.

3. Use plain language, and make your presentation as straightforward as possible. The judges may not be aware of the intricate details of your business niche, and more than likely won't understand any technical or other jargon you might use. Also don't assume they know everything about your industry or merchandise. If you don't have the ability to explain this in simple terms, then find someone who can do it for you.

Takeaways

- Remember to choose the awards you are going to enter very carefully. Out of more than 1,000 awards available, select those that you have the highest chance of winning. Picking the right award, which aligns with your strengths, can give you a probability of success that is 20 percent greater than before you even start writing. Be honest with the judges and yourself about your capabilities, and how you can display them.

- Don't spend too much time thinking about whether or not to participate. The only way to win is to join the competition, so make sure you enter all of the awards which are suitable for you. The more you enter, the more opportunities you have of succeeding.

- Even though you need to demonstrate that your business shines more brightly than all of the others who entered the same category, this doesn't mean that it has to be the best in the whole of the United Kingdom or the world. Simply the most remarkable one, taking part in a specified award.

PART 5

Be the Best Version of You

CHAPTER 17

How I Got Into Time Management

I like everything to be scheduled. This started when I was very young. I used to spend a lot of time at my grandparents' house, and I especially loved being with Grandad Roger.

Unfortunately, he passed away when I was seven years old, but he taught me so much and played a huge part in shaping the person I am today. I learned from him the importance of always being on time, or showing up early. He also supported my passion for radio, and we spent a lot of our time together listening to it. He used to buy me huge packs of blank cassette tapes, so that I could record my favorite programs.

Timing is very important on the radio, and like him, I became obsessed with it. Grandad used to plan every part of his day, even if he wasn't doing very much. That way he always seemed to make the most of every second, and I still follow this strategy now.

It's fine to occasionally have a lazy day, but my version of this is far removed from what some of my friends consider it should be. I was brought up to always dress as if I was going somewhere nice. Not spend time lazing around in pajamas. Even when I was ill as a child, I was still encouraged to get dressed and be smart. Although I do have days now when I am more chilled out, catching up on YouTube videos and television, I find it difficult to sit still in one place for too long. I like to keep busy.

However, I realize that planning everything as much as I do must sometimes irritate my parents and friends, who are more laid back. Whilst I find myself getting anxious if I don't have a plan, am late, or the day isn't moving forward according to my schedule.

I still admire Grandad Roger. He is my hero! Growing up I always knew that if I could only be half of the person he was, I would feel that I had accomplished something amazing.

I realize that this may sound obsessive but my strategies work really well, which is why I want to share them with you.

My Time Management Strategies, and the 80/20 Rule

I don't think that the Pareto Principle, which is also referred to as the 80/20 rule, really matters in the grand scheme of things. It's far more important to acknowledge that a small percentage of the actions we take can result in meaningful progress.

Consider your daily activities. Whether you are working or studying 20 percent of what you do will usually seem to be strenuous, tricky, or dull. These are often essential tasks that will have a huge impact.

In both personal life and work, you might be faced with a long list of things to do. Since it would be impossible to handle all of them at once, you have to decide which one to do first. It is essential that you make the right choice. Utilizing the 80/20 approach when it comes to projects, allows me to focus more on the most important tasks. Hence be more efficient, and productive.

If you are creating a business plan, for example, you need to dedicate 20 percent of your time to outlining your thoughts and ideas. Then getting them into a written format. The remaining 80 percent of your time should be spent in perfecting the details. Such as making modifications, adding appropriate fonts, and headings. The 20 percent of effort you put in upfront will make the rest of the task seem much easier.

Other Strategies That Help Me Stay on Track

These top tips will help you stay in control of your day so that you own your time, and don't let it own you:

1. **Persevere**
   Carry on with what you are doing, and look for ways to deal with pressure, like going for a walk to clear your head.

Also, don't become disillusioned by failure. Take a positive view of this. It may not be the best when it's happening, but ultimately, we learn the most from our mistakes.

2. **Share tasks and problems with others**

Asking for help when you have tried your best, and acknowledging that you will need an extra pair of hands to get the project finished by the deadline, is an important time management skill. Asking for help doesn't make you look weak.

Top tip: Sometimes you have to say no to others, especially if you are short of time!

3. **Avoid procrastination**

The best time to do something is usually NOW. Taking action leads to further action. Staying still, and putting things off leads to inaction!

Organize your work to meet deadlines, and give yourself a reward when you achieve a goal.

4. **Log your time**

Write down everything you do in one week. Identifying those areas of your life where you waste time and could be more efficient, also when you are most productive. Schedule your most demanding tasks for the times when you are most productive.

5. **Take regular breaks**

Get up and move around, at least once an hour, if you are sitting in front of a computer screen or laptop. This will help to refresh your thoughts and ideas.

6. **Create good habits**

Try to do tasks at the same time, and in the same place, each day.

7. **Prioritize**

Do urgent, and important tasks first. Not the easy ones! Have a reminder system so that you are notified when you have got an important deadline or task coming up. Again, you might find using the 80/20 rule helpful in getting the important things done first.

8. **Avoid distractions, and being interrupted when you work**

Keep your desk tidy and make sure you know where everything is that you are likely to need while you are working.

Also, check your e-mails at specific times during the day. If you are getting too many, they distract you from the important stuff.

Steer clear of Facebook, Twitter, and Instagram. These are rewards for achieving your goals. Not part of your daily things-to-do list! Take care of yourself, and don't get caught up in a social media overload.

9. **Action planning**

Set clearly defined goals. Realistic ones that you can achieve. Breaking tasks down into steps, which you can do one at a time.

10. **Keep a to-do list**

A to-do list is a game-changer! So, keep one, and update it every day. Write down deadlines, and emphasize key points.

Top tip: Also have a "done" list, so that you can keep track of your achievements. Believe me! Moving something across to your "done" list can be immensely satisfying.

11. **Review your progress**

Revise your plans, if necessary. Life is constantly changing, so you need to be too. Always have a Plan B in case your main one doesn't work out in the way you expect it to. Whatever your goal is, come up with several routes to achieve it. There isn't a single right way to achieve success.

Resource Management Strategies

I use my phone calendar to block out my time. I have everything I do scheduled in from work and meetings to workouts and cinema trips. The downside to this is that my calendar is often booked up weeks in advance, which makes being spontaneous or moving things around difficult to do.

If I am finding a task difficult, I often take myself away from it for 20 minutes or so. For example, I find cleaning therapeutic. So, if I am stuck on a project, or when writing for a client, I may take a break to vacuum the house before coming back to my desk to try again.

Or I might take my border collie, Nelly, for a walk. This usually makes me feel refreshed and able to get back into what I am working on. It's important to take a break and get a change of scenery if you need it. I used to feel frustrated when my old smartwatch told me to stand up every hour if I was fully focused on my scheduled task, but it was a great reminder to step away from my desk and move around regularly.

Takeaways

- Don't worry if your time management isn't as good as you would like it to be. We aren't born with this skill. It has to be learned and continuously improved.
- Although I use my phone calendar to block out my time, there are other tools you may feel more comfortable with. Like a notebook and pen, online planner, or plenty of time management apps to choose from.
- Remember when I said that spending time on social media is a reward for getting the tasks done, make sure you schedule blocks of time for this. Or whatever else you love doing, and choose as your distraction.
- It's also a good idea to schedule one or more extra blocks of time each week to regroup and catch up. In case, like me, your diary is fully booked and you may not quite have enough time to finish one of your tasks. It'll give you the opportunity to get on track again.

CHAPTER 18

Maximizing Strengths and Getting Support for Your Weaknesses

When you decided to become a business owner, and if you are anything like me, you were drawn to it because of the strengths you had in your chosen area or industry. Even if this was initially only a passion or huge interest in it.

Later on, I discovered the importance of acknowledging my weaknesses and finding a way to use them to my advantage, so that I could reach my full potential. This meant increasing my knowledge of the industry, how my business would fit into it, what I needed to do to make it work, and was truly letting myself in for it. So that I could turn my lack of knowledge and understanding, or this weakness, into a positive attribute. Helping me to minimize its adverse impact and influence, the more I learned and put what I knew into practice.

You certainly don't have to be an expert at everything to be successful. As long as you remain ahead of the game so far as your clients, customers, and employees are concerned. Whilst dealing with your own weaknesses can also help you understand how to become a better leader.

For example, you can ask an accountant to handle your income tax return and contributions. They can not only do the job for you, provide advice, but also answer any questions you might have to help you gain a better understanding of your finances. Running your business with guidance from other professionals or experts is the best way to learn, as you are doing the job.

Take Ownership of Your Business, and Responsibility for Your Decisions

Creating a mindset shift to take ownership of your business, and the decisions you make, is also essential. I have outsourced tasks before now, and the results haven't been as I had hoped. When this happens, it's important to make decisions quickly to fix the problem. Or use your own experience to adapt, and reshape your business, in moving forward from these mistakes.

If a service or product provider is giving you a hard time, or failing to meet deadlines, consider whether this is their doing. Then make a decision based on this, whether or not to carry on working with them. If appropriate, acknowledging that part of the problem was your failure to provide an accurate, or good enough brief. Something which can happen, however, careful you might have been! Did you also check out the supplier beforehand?

Although you may not have had a hand in the issue, assuming responsibility enables you to take charge of the situation. Taking control of, and owning a vulnerable situation, can help you transform it into a powerful stance.

Figure Out What Matters the Most, and Ask Others for an Opinion

It's a well-recognized fact that we are not all the same, and this is surprisingly a positive attribute. Identifying your individual abilities is the first step to being able to take advantage of your talents and make progress in your business. This is especially relevant in today's fast-paced, and multidisciplinary work environment.

We tend to prioritize our own perspective at any given time. What we are excited about, our expertise, and so on. However, the right thing to do, including for yourself, is to start by concentrating on what's best for the business and your customers. Identifying those activities which bring you the most pleasure, and the ones that require the most energy.

So, take a deep dive into what you enjoy, and conversely, the tasks that drain you. Try to eliminate or outsource anything that you really don't want to do. Alternatively, break down these more difficult tasks into smaller chunks, to make them seem more manageable, as I mentioned earlier in the book. Setting up a business as a young entrepreneur involves a lot of trial and error. Tasks you might have enjoyed in the past may also become boring later. It's important to continually assess how you feel about your business tasks, and make decisions based on this.

Any feedback you receive, whether it's given formally or informally, is a gift! High achievers tend to focus mainly on areas that need improvement, but it's equally important to recognize the positive comments as part of both your business and personal growth.

Under-promising and overdelivering are essential to achieving success in business and are values I have always carried with me. It's rewarding when clients say to any of us that we have gone above and beyond what was expected. This is also what keeps me going through the more challenging tasks.

Pay Attention to the Details

I recently visited Disneyland Paris for the first time, and was struck by how many hidden details were everywhere I looked. Throughout the parks, hotels, and restaurants. Everything produced a "wow" response! It was difficult to believe that there could be so much magic, even in unexpected places. Such as the paving stones we were walking on, and cutlery in the restaurants. However, when you look at the most successful companies and entrepreneurs, the majority of them pay impeccable attention to detail.

With this in mind, it's important for business owners to not only identify their weaknesses but also seek support when they are feeling low. I work with a wonderful life and business coach, Helen Campbell, on a six-weekly basis. We chat about everything that has, or hasn't, been going well.

I can't recommend this highly enough. Look for a coach who has experience, excellent listening skills, and in-depth knowledge of what it takes to grow a successful company. Helen has been an instrumental part of my success over the last three years. She listens, with kindness, and without judging me. This support helps me to reach my goals more quickly.

I have undergone counseling and therapy at different stages during my life. Since I have believed for a long time that a good listening ear can be empowering, and instrumental in our success.

Takeaway

- Whether or not you work with a business coach, consider your friendship circles, and who you can count on for support when your energy is low.

CHAPTER 19

Learn From Everything You Do

Go for It! There Are Huge Benefits in Trial and Error

As you know by now, not everything I have tried has been a success, but I still firmly believe that if you have a hobby or passion you want to turn into a business then go for it! If things don't work out, at least you can say you have tried, and you are not left wondering what might have been. No one can be absolutely certain that the risks will pay off, no matter how calculated they might be, but this shouldn't stop you from taking them. If you want your business to succeed, risks play a vital role in this.

If it's become a matter of overthinking a course of action before taking the first step, no one knows how the future will play out or if your business will be successful. However, if you plan ahead, this will help you mitigate the potential for failure. Developing a business strategy, exploring financial scenarios, and revisiting your initial performance are just a few ways you can navigate the unknown. Doing this will at least allow you to be ready, to handle any difficult situations or unexpected changes which might come along.

An optimistic risk-taker always regard failure as an opportunity to learn. Since it teaches us how to think, and plan strategically for future projects. This belief should be integral to the way you do business, alongside a system that will enable you to analyze performance.

Remember too that we are living in an ever-changing world, and whatever industry we are in, the impact of this will affect us to a lesser or greater extent. When you combine the effect of this with the fact that our customers will have constantly changing demands, it results in consistent opportunities for new business. Innovation is vitally important for entrepreneurs. Whilst success ultimately involves sharing, and teaching what we know. Also putting new ideas into practice to achieve continual progress.

Since a lot of people tend to avoid taking risks, those who are brave enough to do so have a competitive advantage of there being less competition. This means that if you have found a worthwhile opportunity, and no one else has jumped on it, you will be the only business reaping the benefits of it.

For this reason, whenever you are wondering whether to take a risk, keep your competitors in mind. If you don't, they may opt to grab the opportunity you have allowed to slip away. As I mentioned earlier, provided you have calculated the risk in the best way you can and understand the potential return, this should give you an idea of whether or not taking it has the potential to be worthwhile.

Reflection Is a Necessity

I have developed a successful career by stepping outside of my comfort zone and building a solid foundation from which I can continue to grow. If I hadn't entered the school enterprise competition in the first place, my business may never have come into existence. If I hadn't been through so much bullying, I might not have felt as if I had to prove myself by becoming successful. Whilst self-employment wasn't anywhere on my radar, as a young child.

Reflection, or thinking as deeply as you can about your business and personal life, is a very important skill to have. It has helped me a lot in the past to take the next step, be able to move forward, and continue to do so. On the other hand, I have always found new year's resolutions frustrating. Quite simply, we don't need a new year to make positive changes in our lives. Reflection isn't just the thing you do when December fades into the next year. It's a vitally important practice to cultivate and grow, all year long. Especially for an entrepreneur, or someone who wants to be successful in his or her career.

Here are a few of the advantages I have discovered from taking the time to reflect:

- It's helpful in recognizing our own abilities, qualities, and feelings. Giving us a greater sense of self-awareness, and how this affects our behavior and decision making.
- We also get a better understanding of our own values and beliefs. So that we can step back and analyze a situation objectively.

Disregarding our own preferences enables us to provide clear and unbiased advice. So better assistance to our teams, customers, and partners. Even if this should mean accepting that ours may not be the most suitable business to address their needs, and we ought to refer customers or clients to a competitor.

- Self-assessment can lead to progress and potential growth. Also, the achievement of goals.
- We can avoid professional stagnation by analyzing and refining arning and improve our practices. Encouraging us to remain committed to innovation and not only rely on traditional techniques.

How to Manage Your Self-Reflection

At the end of every day, take a few minutes to make a note of anything that happened that still stands out in your thoughts. Whether it's a positive, or negative occurrence. It might include something you felt strongly about or a situation you didn't manage as well as you believe you could have done. This will give you the opportunity to analyze, and rationalize, your opinion about the incident. Also, consider any changes to your practices which might have created a different or better result. If it wasn't the one you were hoping for, take you any nearer to achieving a goal, or didn't support your values.

Gratitude is another important tool, which can be accessed through reflection. I journal every morning and evening. Listing three things I am grateful for each time I do it, and every evening, what I would change about my day if this is possible. This helps me to show and express gratitude regularly. As an important reflective practice, it allows me to improve what I intend to do the following day, if I need to. Or consider how I might also give back to others.

Failure Has the Potential to Become a Huge, Superpower Success

My success has come from life-long failures and hard work. I could easily have been a nobody. I was bullied throughout my education, and some of my teachers didn't believe in me. I could have had an average career, achieved average grades, and coasted along. Not making anything of myself. Nevertheless, my strategy was to turn this negativity into my superpower. When I felt like a failure in the darkest of days, and the bullying was at its worst, I knew that I had to prove all of them wrong. ...This is where my power came from.

Few people think of failure as a superpower. I do, because it has been a major factor in my accomplishments. The secret lies in my aptitude to fail, expeditiously. The faster I fail, the more my determination to succeed increases, and my superpower is enhanced.

Think about your life so far, for a moment. Recall a time when you didn't do well at something. What more than likely sprung to mind was something you hadn't done before. Do you recognize the underlying message? Even though you may have failed, it implies that you were willing to give it a shot. To put yourself in a vulnerable position. You left your comfort zone and took on something which made you feel anxious, might well have frightened you, and ultimately challenged you.

Reflect on this experience when you failed. What did you take away from it? I am certain that you will have learned quite a bit. You may have identified approaches that were unhelpful or discovered more about yourself. Take a long hard look at this incident until you have found your key.

However, the most significant takeaway from it will be what you have done with the information you gained. How was it implemented into your life? What kind of transformation have you gone through? What are doing now that is unlike before?

It's not that I REALLY ENJOY messing up but I still take pleasure in reflecting on all of my mistakes, figuring out what I have learned from each one, and looking at how it has altered my course.

As I have grown older, I realize that I fail more quickly. This helps me gain knowledge faster, which in turn allows me to pivot and try something new. By changing course quickly, I am able to achieve my desired results faster. Do you follow the logic?

In order to fail fast, it is important not to overanalyze the situation. Instead of spending six months deliberating on a new endeavor, it's more effective to dive in. Allow yourself to make mistakes, learn from them, and keep going. At the end of six months, you will be much farther along than if you had spent all of that time worrying and seeking perfection.

I am going to issue a challenge: Take something that you have had an interest in doing and pursue it! Don't wait until you feel comfortable, and sure of yourself. Just jump in now. RIGHT NOW! If you don't succeed, don't worry. It's still better than not trying at all.

The secret is to remember that you can't get stuck in your failures. Unless you allow yourself to. Instead, ask what you can learn from the experience, and how you can move on.

Therein lies your superpower. Go on.... Use it!

Takeaways

- Reflection is hugely beneficial, easy to do, and can lead to powerful results. Far outweighing the time, you spend on it.
- I had to be brave on my darkest of days, to turn my weaknesses and failures into a superpower for success. It wasn't easy, but I promise that you are brave too. Being brave is knowing that somewhere deep inside of you, the courage to carry on will be there when you need it. Whether or not you can feel it now. I promise you.... It is there.

CHAPTER 20

Maintaining Positive Mental Health

You Need a Healthy Work–Life Balance for Great Mental Health

Looking after my mental health has always been important to me, and even more so since I started working on this book. At the beginning of 2023, I discovered that I had a heart condition after suffering from high blood pressure and chest pains. It was a scary time, trying to navigate how this would affect my daily activities and life generally. Also, a sharp reminder that I did need to slow down a little.

Being self-employed comes with a lot of freedom, but it has its drawbacks too. For instance, when I go on holiday, I still struggle with being able to completely switch off. Although I have found it easier over the last few years to park my work, and put it to the back of my mind. Especially since I have been able to use a virtual assistant to look after my e-mail inbox. Nevertheless, there are still times on holiday when I might have to pick something up. I obviously try to avoid doing this if I can, and the majority of my clients don't contact me unless it's an emergency.

Even worse, my family has sometimes found it difficult to deal with me not being able to spend time with them when it was supposed to be a holiday. The time I have with my family is very precious, and important, to me. The same applies to my friends. When I am having a great time with them, I still sometimes have to take a work call, reply to an e-mail, or WhatsApp a client. Not only that, any leave I do take means that I have to make sure all of my work is wrapped up before I go away, which always makes the week leading up to the holiday incredibly stressful.

Dealing With Stress, and Burnout

Even though it has taken me a long time to realize this, the longer I have been self-employed the clearer it has become.... Work really can wait! Making memories with loved ones, and good friends, is far more important. As a result, I have been making certain that I am always present when it comes to enjoying my free time, because in the past my thoughts have often been elsewhere. My family is everything to me, so they should always come first.

However, not everyone appreciates or understands this. Similarly, it has become one of my personal boundaries. After thinking about it for a long time, I also came to realize that if clients don't respect my need for a reasonable amount of time away from work, we are not unfortunately a good fit. Meaning that I should cut my ties with them. Furthermore, it's important not to lose sight of the fact that money is a commodity. The flow of it comes and goes when you are in business. Whereas if you miss the opportunity to make memories with your family and friends, you won't get this time back again.

Working in social media and digital marketing means that I spend the majority of my time online, and I often find it hard to relax at home. The cinema takes me away from my phone, and other distractions. So, it has always been my happy place. It's what I do to unwind completely and enjoy the escapism for a few hours.

When I was growing up my parents used to take me to see movies regularly. I thought of it then as a safe haven. While I was going through a lot of trauma and tough times, because of being bullied at school. The other kids used to play football, or another sport at the weekend, but I always looked forward to seeing the latest movies. I feel incredibly fortunate now to have had these fantastic experiences when I was growing up.

I also found that listening to music was a great help in keeping my mental health good and being brought up with a lot of different varieties. So much so that I struggle now to work without it playing in the background. It's great motivation and can soon take my mind off any problems I might have.

You also need to maintain regular working hours. Don't respond to e-mails or WhatsApp messages outside of this time. Your clients will come to regard this as normal. E-mail scheduling tools are great for sending replies during working hours. If you are setting up self-employment alongside a full-time job, it's important to constantly assess how you are feeling, whether you are still getting enough time for yourself, and the right amount of sleep! If you are already doing a full-time job and taking on more work in your spare time, it can soon have a negative impact on your personal and social life.

It is very tempting to try to devote every available second you have to work. Especially when you are excited about getting started or need to bring in extra income to cover your bills, but this carries a massive risk of burnout. Even more so when you have also forgotten to take into account the extra time needed for admin, and other responsibilities you will have when you work for yourself.

How to Recognize Burnout

Burnout is a serious condition. It can cause you to have an aversion to work so that you no longer want to do it! Irrespective of how much you enjoyed it earlier and your productivity can suffer.

It affects people in different ways, but the list of symptoms usually includes:

- Feeling exhausted most of the time, even after you have just woken up.
- Your immune system is low, and you are often ill.
- Frequent headaches, muscle pain, indigestion, and stomach problems.
- An increased sense of self-doubt, fear of failure, or imposter syndrome.
- Feeling trapped, defeated, and helpless. Even when you are looking at small problems.
- A sense of isolation and detachment.
- Lack of motivation, or not wanting to do anything.
- A negative outlook, being cynical, and not getting as much satisfaction when you do manage to complete a task.
- Procrastination, avoiding, and withdrawing from responsibilities.
- Becoming irritable and frustrated more easily.

What to Do If Everything Does Get on Top of You

These symptoms need to be taken seriously before they have an even greater impact on your health, and it's important to speak to a medical professional. Even though once you are in a state of burnout, you are probably finding it difficult to care and believe that any positive change will be unlikely.

Setting boundaries for yourself during burnout is very important. Communicating these to clients and customers will help to ensure that you are not overpromising unrealistic expectations, then underdelivering. For example, taking private client phone calls during your employed hours could soon cause issues with your employer. Whilst ignoring them might understandably lead to frustration, if you haven't explained to your clients that you will be unavailable at specific times.

Conversely, still working flat out may sometimes be unavoidable during emergencies, but this will probably only be sustainable in the short term. Otherwise, you will soon feel the full impact of it on your health, social life, and personal relationships.

One of the benefits of becoming self-employed alongside an existing job is that this can prove your business does have the potential to be successful, before you decide to go all-in with it. Setting clear boundaries on your part-time career also makes it simpler to prioritize your full-time employment, which is likely to be your main source of income in the early days.

At the outset when you are considering freelancing or self-employment around a full-time job, the first step will be to identify what is important to you personally. In addition to your working hours, you might have existing family commitments, important hobbies, or responsibilities which will also demand some of your time.

It's important at this point to know what your goal is. So, ask yourself the following questions, and take time to answer them:

- Are you aiming to build a new business empire and move to full-time self-employment?
- Do you intend to treat your self-employment as a sustainable extra income stream?

- Will freelancing simply give you the opportunity to explore new skills, possibly an existing passion, and bring in a little extra money at the same time?

This will give you a clearer picture of how much time you can or should realistically spend on your self-employed work, and what you may need to sacrifice to reach the goal you have set. For example, you might want to get up earlier to do any freelance work you have before taking your children to school and heading to your full-time job. This could mean skipping weekday gym visits for a while.

Alternatively, you could find that by cutting down on watching television in the evening or playing video games, this will free up enough time to devote to your new business. While still being able to schedule regular time, with your partner or family.

Investing in a separate computer and mobile phone for your self-employed business will avoid any contractual issues in using equipment supplied by your employer. Also prevent the risk of accidentally tweeting from a company account by mistake, or your boss having access to your freelancing accounts.

Spending extra time on work needs to be financially rewarding, whether it's a short-term gain or to achieve a bigger monetary benefit in the long run. As a result, you need to know exactly how much you are earning from your employed career, and how to set realistic freelancing rates, to make the extra effort worthwhile. Also, set targets and goals for your self-employed business, to know when it's financially viable.

Having goals and targets like this means that you will soon know if you are heading in the right direction and should eventually move into self-employment full-time. Alternatively, if what you are doing is another useful income stream, enjoyable activity, or skill that is worth pursuing.

Finally, always try to be realistic about your limits. Self-employment isn't the right career option for everyone, and you might decide that you would prefer to focus on a full-time job rather than quit one to become a professional freelancer. Or you might, for instance, need to pause what you are doing to allow family and friends to take priority for a while.

One of the biggest advantages of working for yourself is having the control, and capability, to make these decisions. However, you will only be able to choose the best option if you can see things impartially, or by getting external opinions and advice.

Takeaways

- If you want to build a sustainable freelancing business it's important to schedule time away from work to relax and help you maintain a healthy work–life balance.
- Also, find something you really love and ensure that you make time for it. Unless you keep up your passions, and take some downtime, you can start to resent your work and won't be as invested in it.
- Having confidence, and belief in what you are doing, is very important when you start working for yourself. Also, being able to admit that you find something too difficult to do. This is the first step in tackling the problem.

CHAPTER 21

Dealing With the Impact of Negativity

Unfortunately, jealousy could be something you will experience in business, as I did. Given how common it is. Along with toxic relationships, and others who don't have the self-awareness to realize how destructive and damaging their behavior can be.

As you already know, I faced a lot of friction from some of the students and teachers at school when I started my business. It was very upsetting at the time and affected my mental health. Nevertheless, I was succeeding at something I loved, supported by friends and family who only wanted the best for me, and I wasn't doing anything wrong. Whereas the students and teachers concerned were coming from a negative place, from which they felt comfortable showing their hate.

I expect they also didn't like that I was proving them wrong. Despite how hard they tried, I wasn't prepared to give up. Why did I need to, when I was capable of making something of my life? Although I didn't realize it at the time, I was following my purpose, so doing what was right for me.

I obviously didn't want this to happen, or be the recipient of their unacceptable behavior. Where was the kindness in what they did? I realize now that people who behave in this way often want to copy our success, but they don't know how to ask for help to empower themselves.

At the time, I felt that the only option I had at school was to push through, and discard those opinions which I came to the conclusion didn't matter. Since they were coming from a place of unkindness, a very negative stance, and a bad attitude. I am not saying it was easy, but I was very fortunate to be able to turn what could have been a disaster into the foundation of a career I have grown to love.

However, experiencing others' negativity still occasionally happens to me today, in business and my freelance work. Mostly when dealing with new clients, who were never going to be a good fit for my skills or the services I offer, but which wasn't apparent at the outset. I would also like to include here the considerable online abuse I received after I came to Zoella's defense. Remember what happened when I raised my profile, through the media attention my blog article received?

Combating Bullying, Jealousy, or Other Toxic Behavior

Here are some of the ways you can do this:

1. **Try to change your opinion of toxic people**

   I know how difficult this can be, but I promise it helps if you can do it. Not only do bullies tend to express negative emotions, but also they are usually very unhappy in themselves, often confused. Releasing their anger on the nearest person, because of how bad they are feeling. If you can think of it like this, what they are doing isn't actually about you.

   Whatever the reason might be, it's very important not to dwell on it. Instead, try to use others' negativity as motivation to succeed even better and more frequently, as I did at school. While I listened to, and took constructive criticism on board, from those who did have my best interests at heart.

   All of us are unique. I am young, self-motivated, and outspoken. I am also gay. I made the decision early on to use others' negativity to fuel my ongoing success, since I felt this was the right thing for me to do. It enabled, and empowered me, to move on with my life.

2. **Remember your purpose**

   When someone's anger, hate, or bitterness is directed at you, try to look at the situation objectively. If you are still following your purpose, and haven't made a mistake, you are on the right track.

   When someone personally attacks me now, I take a step back, check as quickly as I can that I haven't inadvertently done anything wrong, and use what they are saying as feedback which I can use to my advantage.

Always remember what you have been called to do, who you are, and how you got there. When you do this, jealousy, and bad feeling, should have less of an impact on you. It will instead make you stronger.

3. **Keep on improving**

The only person you are in competition with is yourself. Even though some people will try their hardest to take you down, you must carry on improving. This isn't to show that you are better than them but to prove you are better than YOU.

Work on yourself until your haters ask you if you are hiring. When they ask for the job, make them prove themselves ten times harder, before you consider giving it to them. ...Let your success speak for itself!

4. **Ignore Them**

Jealous and toxic people can be difficult to ignore. However, if you get into the habit of blocking them, it can become easier to do. I was hesitant at first to block anyone. I thought that they might be offended, or I could be missing out in some way. Secretly, I was hoping that they might think about what they were doing, and change for the better. Despite how unlikely it was that this would happen. After a while, I realized that it was far better to simply tell people like this, that I didn't want anything more to do with them.

Alternatively, if they make a comment online, don't retaliate in an attempt to give them a dose of their own medicine. All this will do is take you down to their level and could end up making matters worse for you.

Remember you always have a choice in how you deal with a situation like this. Where family and friends are concerned you can block them, ignore them, or confront them with love.

5. **Communicate your boundaries before you start work**

If you are freelancing, offering a service or product, set out all of your business terms and conditions in an agreement or contract before you start work. Making it perfectly clear what you will do, or provide, for an agreed fee. For instance, the number of hours you are prepared to work each week, the revisions you will do, the date when payment will be due, and so on.

If a client or customer becomes upset or annoyed later then you will have a written record to refer them to. It's very important to remain professional throughout the dispute, and not lash out in your defense. As this can again, make matters worse.

However, if after going through everything with the client or customer he or she is still not happy, it could be that you are simply not a good fit. For instance, he or she may expect you to do an unreasonable amount of extra work when this wasn't part of your initial agreement and will take you a long time to complete. Or is putting you under pressure to comply with unreasonable requests.

This can obviously be very upsetting, especially since time for a freelancer is one of his or her greatest assets. If the client or customer refuses to meet you halfway in resolving the issue, the best option will be to let them go.

Everyone gets bad clients or customers at some point, and the only thing to do is learn from the experience.

6. **Surround yourself with positive people**

I feel grateful every day to have some of the most inspirational, good, and positive people around me. I wouldn't call it a "tribe" but we certainly look out for one another and support each other in any way we can. All of them raise me up. We complement each other and celebrate each other's achievements.

Having positive, and healthy, relationships with the people in your closest circles is crucial for success. I am also very fortunate to have built up a lot of brilliant professional contacts, as part of my business network, so I always know who my cheerleaders will be.

If you need to redefine your circles, make a list of the top three people you would like to delete because of their negativity or bad attitude. Also, look at who you are following on social media, and regularly unfollow anyone who doesn't support your personal values.

Believe me! Clearing out any negativity on your social media is highly therapeutic.

What I Have Learnt About Positivity

- Positivity and happiness are contagious. Other people's emotions rub off on us and impact the way we feel. Have you ever walked into a room full of vibrant, bubbly, and smiling people then instantly felt positive? I know I have done it many times. Even if previously, I hadn't been feeling all that fabulous. Similarly, have you ever found yourself surrounded by a group of negative, unhappy, and fed-up people? Whereas if you choose to be in the company of happy, and motivated, people you won't be able to stop yourself from soaking up some of that amazing positivity!

- The most successful people are those who have a happy, healthy, and positive approach to life. Happiness and positivity influence success. Don't get me wrong! There is much more to being successful in business, and life than that. Nevertheless, those who are happy and healthy in themselves, both physically and emotionally, often achieve more. Feeling down, unhealthy, and sluggish will only leave you super unmotivated and feeling pretty darn rubbish. Conversely when you feel good, you usually also feel unstoppable. It's like having a permanent "spring" in your step, all year around!

- Positive people will inspire you, and you will inspire them. Those you can look at and think how great they are, which is the reason why they are in your life. Whether you work at home by yourself, or in an office full of people, being connected to others who inspire you will fuel your fire. Along with the desire to become a better version of yourself. However, if you are surrounded by people whom you constantly find yourself metaphorically rolling your eyes at, you will most likely sink into a bit of a slump and flatline as a result. ...The secret is to soar, not settle!

- Being "good" is fantastic for the soul. So, choose to surround yourself with "good" people. Those who support charitable or other good causes, don't do anything illegal, and are kind. It will encourage and inspire you to become a better person. On the other hand, if you are surrounded by people who are careless, thoughtless, break the law, feel it's acceptable to litter, and so on this behavior will have the potential to adversely affect your lifestyle. Don't allow this to happen! Being "good" doesn't mean you will be boring. Simply a better person.

- Positive people are grateful, so be grateful! Successful people often say that gratitude is the key to success, and I believe that's true. Think about what you are grateful for. Are you grateful for your friends? Your family? The opportunities life has given you? There is so much we can be thankful for, from the smallest to the more significant things.

Receiving Advice From Others

I regularly turn to my friends and professional network when I need help or have a query, but it's important to consider any advice you are given by others before you act on it. I have worked with numerous mentors over the years, and not all of the advice I have been given has been right for me. Starting a business can be overwhelming, especially when people offer you a lot of "helpful" suggestions. Remember that while your business may have similarities to theirs, your approach to management, and problem solving is likely to be different. For instance, does what they are suggesting match your goals, or where you would like to be in five years?

Instead of simply trying to take the advice you have received, and keep everyone happy, concentrate instead on resolving the issues you asked them about. With your business plan, and vision for the future, firmly in mind. Ultimately the choices that you make, and the outcome of any problems you have, are your responsibility. Your business is unique, and any outside advice has the potential to alter your perspective. So be wary of this, and confident in your own decision making.

When working with a mentor, it's also a good idea to take a close look at his or her viewpoint. To ensure that the guidance which is being given matches your goals. For example, it may be based on building your business quickly, with a view to selling it. Or focused on slow, and steady growth, to create a business that stands the test of time. Whilst any advice, or help you receive from a mentor, should be based on what you are ultimately looking to do.

Takeaways

- If you are being bullied, or subjected to someone else's toxic behavior, this isn't your fault!

- Listen, and action constructive advice or criticism, received from those who do have your best interests at heart.
- The best people to surround yourself with are the ones who have a positive mindset and regularly practice gratitude.
- Always remember that you are not alone! If the bullying is getting you down, talk to someone you trust. Like a parent or other family member, teacher, or friend. You don't have to go through this on your own.
- Remember too that I am with you! I go into schools to talk about bullying, work with charities, and other organizations who can help. I know what it felt like when I was bullied at school, and I want to stop this from happening to others.

PART 6

Planning for the Future

I hope you have enjoyed reading my story so far, and that you found this book helpful. Especially if you are considering how to become a successful entrepreneur.

There was a time when I hadn't even thought of being self-employed, as a Digital Marketing Consultant. It's been a huge journey, and I am so grateful for all of the wonderful opportunities I have had. Also, the people I met along the way, or who shared my path even for a short time.

I am looking forward to whatever comes next. Including spending more quality time with my family, friends, and Nelly!

What I Would Like to Do Next

I plan to carry on helping as many people as I can, to achieve success in their careers, and businesses. Right now, I am focused on stepping up my charity work with Youth Employment UK. After volunteering with them since 2016, I want to do everything I can to ensure the organization continues to flourish and empowers young people by tackling youth unemployment. A cause I wholeheartedly support.

I would still love to land my own radio show. My passion for it hasn't faded, and continuing to explore opportunities in this area is something else I plan to do.

I want to take more vacations. I recently took my first solo trip, and it was a wonderful experience. Not having a partner, I used to think that I wouldn't enjoy having a break by myself. Now I want to explore all of the places on my bucket list, and why not? Something else I have learned along the way is that life really is an adventure. We need to make the most of it, and not forget to have fun.

Feeling Grateful

I have made mistakes, struggled with challenges, and sometimes failed. Also been laughed at, and told to quit. However, what got me through the most difficult times was learning from the things I did wrong. Helped to get back on track by the support, inspiration, and motivation of others who wanted me to do well. A huge thank you to you from the bottom of my heart. I couldn't have done it without you!

I would also like to say a big thank you to those who bullied me. Although you made my life upsetting and difficult, you inspired my success without even realizing it. If I hadn't been in such a dark place because of your actions, I don't believe that I would be where I am today.

Speaking and writing are two of the ways I have found to pay forward what I have learned. So that business owners, entrepreneurs, and other young people can avoid the same pitfalls I encountered and go on to achieve great things. Writing this book has been a huge challenge and something I have wanted to do for a long time. So, I will always be grateful to my publisher, Business Expert Press, for helping me make it happen.

I also have other books now I would like to write, and a lot of ideas based on developing e-learning resources, to continue paying forward everything I learned. In the hope that this will inspire others to do their best work.

Believe You Can, and You Will!

If, like myself, you were told that you couldn't be successful I hope that this book is the proof you need. To show you that you can be anything you want to be, and nothing is truly impossible (unless medical considerations prevent it).

The best advice I can leave you with is.... To always believe in yourself. If you don't, you will be limiting what you can do, and the opportunities that will come your way.

This is one of my favorite quotes from Bob Proctor (1934 to 2022):

The only limits in life are those we impose on ourselves.

Thank you for purchasing a copy of this book. It means a lot to me and inspires me to carry on writing. I am looking forward to sharing the next stage of my journey with you.

I know you will already be successful in many different ways that you may not have realized. Also, you are incredibly brave. Setting up a business isn't a small feat. The fact that you are exploring your ideas, or have already started, is brilliant!

Know that I am right behind you, every step of the way.... On this fantastic journey.

All the very best,
Harvey.

About the Author

Harvey Morton is a multi-award-winning Digital Marketing Consultant, writer, podcaster, and public speaker based in Sheffield. He lives with Nelly, a fantastic Border Collie dog.

Harvey attributes his personal and business success to persistence, learning how to overcome obstacles when he failed, and the superpower belief that he really could be an entrepreneur.

His mission is to help other young people succeed in business, or a career they are passionate about. A circle of family, friends, and supporters share his whirlwind adventure.

Index

OTHER TITLES IN THE BUSINESS CAREER DEVELOPMENT COLLECTION

Vilma Barr, Consultant, Editor

- *Still Room for Humans* by Stan Schatt
- *Am I Doing This Right?* by Tony D. Thelen, Matthew C. Mitchell and Jeffrey A. Kappen
- *Telling Your Story, Building Your Brand* by Henry Wong
- *Social Media Is About People* by Cassandra Bailey and Dana M. Schmidt
- *Pay Attention!* by Cassandra M. Bailey and Dana M. Schmidt
- *Remaining Relevant* by Karen Lawson
- *The Road to Champagne* by Alejandro Colindres Frañó
- *Burn Ladders. Build Bridges* by Alan M. Patterson
- *Decoding Your STEM Career* by Peter J. Devenyi
- *The Networking Playbook* by Darryl L. Howes
- *The Street-Smart Side of Business* by Tara Acosta
- *Rules Don't Work for Me* by Gail Summers
- *How to Use Marketing Techniques to Get a Great Job* by Edward Barr
- *Fast Forward Your Career* by Simonetta Lureti and Lucio Furlani

Concise and Applied Business Books

The Collection listed above is one of 30 business subject collections that Business Expert Press has grown to make BEP a premiere publisher of print and digital books. Our concise and applied books are for...

- Professionals and Practitioners
- Faculty who adopt our books for courses
- Librarians who know that BEP's Digital Libraries are a unique way to offer students ebooks to download, not restricted with any digital rights management
- Executive Training Course Leaders
- Business Seminar Organizers

Business Expert Press books are for anyone who needs to dig deeper on business ideas, goals, and solutions to everyday problems. Whether one print book, one ebook, or buying a digital library of 110 ebooks, we remain the affordable and smart way to be business smart. For more information, please visit www.businessexpertpress.com, or contact sales@businessexpertpress.com.

www.ingramcontent.com/pod-product-compliance
Lightning Source LLC
Chambersburg PA
CBHW061322220326
41599CB00026B/4985

* 9 7 8 1 6 3 7 4 2 5 3 7 4 *